365 DAYS

A GUIDE TO HEALING, IMPROVING RELATIONSHIPS, AND SPIRITUAL GROWTH

365 DAYS

A GUIDE TO HEALING, IMPROVING RELATIONSHIPS, AND SPIRITUAL GROWTH

JENNIFER ONSTOT, MA, MFT

DEDICATION

To my children Declan and Chloe who have deepened my experience of being human and inspired me to continual growth.

Acknowledgments

The author wishes to thank and acknowledge the following individuals:

Kim Abernathy

Lisa Angel

Jill Bailey

Ceci Edith

Stephanie Hammer

Pennisue Hignell

Tabitha Ledford

Joanna Miller

Chloe Onstot

Declan Onstot

Justin Onstot

Wendy Robinson

JoAnne Shelton

Ray Shelton

And the wonderful people with whom
I sit and journey every day

How to Use This Book

This book is intended as a year-long exercise. I recommend that you journal as you go along. I have a personal habit of journaling, and it is one way of processing thoughts and feelings and gaining greater objectivity, clarification, and resolve. Ideally, you would read the meditation the first day, and allow yourself some time to ponder it. Then you would re-read it each day, with time to answer the question associated with that day. Learning is generally a process that requires repetition, so reading the meditation 7 days in a row is by design. Of course, some will go faster, and some will go slower, and some will stop and then start again later. None of these will impede your exploration if you are open.

The meditations and questions in this book are written to provoke deep and comprehensive thought, as well as an assessment of how your past has shaped your present, and how you can reshape your future. If you find yourself, at any time, overwhelmed by a particular question or meditation, that would be a good time to reach out to a support person or perhaps to a professional. You could always skip questions that are particularly overwhelming or come back to them another time. Treat yourself well and gently in this process. A component of strength is having an awareness of our limitations. These exercises are meant to be a gentle and honoring stretch, not like being on a rack. Relax and enjoy the process - time with yourself to come to greater awareness, knowledge, and acceptance.

Above all else, know that these words were written with care, and intended to be gracious. Know that there is not meant to be any judgment or harshness associated with these words. We all need healthy helpings of patience, generosity, love, and grace as we journey and grow.

This book is not intended to replace or conflict with personalized, professional advice.

TABLE OF CONTENT

Dedication...5

Acknowledgments...7

How to Use This Book...9

Shame: *Week 1* 15

Memories: *Week 2* 21

Honesty: *Week 3* 27

Fail with Dignity: *Week 4*...33

Letting go of Expectations: *Week 5*..............................39

Realistic Long-term Relationship Vows: *Week 6*.......45

On Grieving: *Week 7*...51

Tiny Steps: *Week 8* 57

Confrontations: *Week 9* 63

More Grieving: *Week 10*..69

Control: *Week 11* 75

Holding Two Things: *Week 12*..81

Hold Onto Hope: *Week 13* 87

Unprocessed Negative Feelings: *Week 14* 93

Two Worlds: *Week 15* 101

Uninspired: *Week 16* 107

Do for Yourself: *Week 17* 113

Firm Edges, Flexible Center: *Week 18* 119

Death: *Week 19* 125

Power Out: *Week 20* 131

Waiting: *Week 21* 137

Never Say "Never": *Week 22* 143

The Importance of Rejection: *Week 23* 149

The Perfect Relationship: *Week 24* 155

One Whole: *Week 25* 161

Every Moment: *Week 26* 167

Good and Bad: *Week 27* 173

Saying Goodbye: *Week 28* 179

Speaking Up: *Week 29* 185

Just Breathe: *Week 30* 191

Life Teachers: *Week 31* 197

The Snuckle: *Week 32* 203

Be the Butterfly: *Week 33* 209

Whole Person: *Week 34* 215

Comparing: *Week 35* 221

Grateful: *Week 36* 227

Worth: *Week 37* 233

More is More: *Week 38* 239

Our Stories Matter: *Week 39* 245

Let's Play: *Week 40* 251

Yin Yang: *Week 41* 257

See the Vision: *Week 42* 263

Face the Hill: *Week 43* 269

The Three Loves: *Week 44* 275

Bitterness: *Week 45* 283

Confessions: *Week 46* 289

Past, Future, Present: *Week 47* 295

Embrace Failure: *Week 48* 301

Embracing True Wealth: *Week 49* 307

Praise, Thanksgiving, Confession, and
Supplication: *Week 50*...313

Trust: *Week 51* 321

Evidence of Love: *Week 52* 327

Understood: *Bonus 1* 333

Hold: *Bonus 2* 339

Theoretically Unlovable: *Bonus 3* 345

Endings: *Bonus 4*..353

Urgent Plea! 355

SHAME

WEEK 1

"Natural shame" is when we feel bad about making a mistake. We feel embarrassed when we make a mistake, such as forgetting to set an alarm or arriving late for an appointment. We might feel flushed. We might feel the blood rush through us. The purpose of natural shame is to make us aware of something we might do differently in the future.

"Learned shame" is when we feel bad about who we are. Learned shame might feel similar in our bodies to natural shame, but it is different. Learned shame is when we think we are not as good as someone else. When we feel learned shame, we might think we are ugly, worthless, or bad. As its name implies, learned shame is a shame that we learned from the people in our lives, who in turn, learned it from the people in their lives.

Learned shame needs to be healed. While natural shame may lead us to growth, learned shame doesn't. Learned shame keeps us preoccupied with ourselves and leaves us unavailable to connect with, and to love, others. Fortunately, there are steps to heal learned shame. We start by noticing the shame without judgment. We feel compassion for ourselves because it is hard to have those feelings about ourselves. Imagine holding the shame in your arms like a little baby. Say kind and nurturing phrases like, "You are lovable, and it is okay to have feelings." We repeat those steps as long as it takes for the shame to subside. When the shame subsides, we are freed up to love ourselves and others. The next time we feel learned shame, we do those steps again.

Today, we will begin to explore and begin to heal learned shame.

Day 1

Close your eyes and think about what you have just read. What are the first couple of things you notice about this meditation?

_____

_____

_____

_____

_____

_____

Day 2

How does your body feel when you experience a significant shame reaction?

_____

_____

_____

_____

_____

_____

Day 3

Can you think of anyone, early in your life, who modeled "learned shame" or directed it at you?

_____

_____

_____

_____

_____

_____

Day 4

What shame statements do you hear in your head, e.g. "I'm no good. I'm not good enough. I don't deserve…?"

_____

_____

_____

_____

_____

_____

Day 5

What would you like to hear in your head instead, e.g. "I'm fine as I am. I am good enough. I deserve love, etc...." You may even write them on a notecard and put them on your bathroom mirror.

_____

_____

_____

_____

_____

Day 6

Say aloud in the mirror your loving statements from yesterday. Say them from a second person perspective, e.g. "You are fine as you are." Note that the discomfort will go away over time. Practice them often over this year.

_____

_____

_____

_____

_____

Day 7

Reflect on what you have learned about yourself this week.

_____

_____

_____

_____

_____

_____

MEMORIES

WEEK 2

All that we are today comes from our personalities, experiences, and memories. The ways we feel and respond come from these processes as well. Memory orients us to life. Memory is functional as long as it is fluid, adaptable, and flexible. We know that healthy memories shift somewhat over time. A mother somewhat forgets the pain of childbirth. If something is really wonderful to us, we ask ourselves "of what does that wonderful feeling remind me?" If something is surprisingly bothersome, we look to the past and ask ourselves when we have felt or experienced something like that before. If we are stuck with a memory that is bothering us, we see if we can tolerate sitting with that memory. We comfort ourselves with phrases like "It's over. I am now free. I am now loved." We might want to give ourselves a hug. We may feel ourselves begin to calm down. We may need to revisit that memory several times. We might talk about the memory with a friend. If there is a memory that feels too big to do this on our own, we seek out professional help.

Today, we begin exploring, accepting, and healing memories.

Day 1

Close your eyes and think about what you just read. What are the first couple of things you notice about this meditation?

_____

_____

_____

_____

_____

_____

Day 2

Can you recall your first memory?

_____

_____

_____

_____

_____

_____

Day 3

What is your worst childhood memory?

_____

_____

_____

_____

_____

_____

Day 4

What is your best childhood memory?

_____

_____

_____

_____

_____

_____

Day 5

Can you cultivate compassion for yourself about your worst childhood memory? What comforting words would you like to say to yourself about that memory (it was not your fault, it's over now…)?

_____

_____

_____

_____

_____

Day 6

How have you grown in your life or become stronger as a result of one of your childhood memories?

_____

_____

_____

_____

_____

_____

Day 7

Reflect on what you have learned about yourself this week. What is an improvement you notice?

_____

_____

_____

_____

_____

_____

HONESTY

WEEK 3

Honesty is an important quality in every relationship. In close relationships, honesty is about sharing; to be known as we truly are. Honesty is not about getting the other person to do what we want. Honesty is not about releasing our anger or changing the other person. We don't have to share everything. We always get to choose how much and when we share. It is healthy and helpful to choose what we share. It is also sad when we go through a relationship and realize the other person only knows or values us as an image of we want them to see. It also creates shame because we are giving ourselves the message, "I'm not worth knowing as I am." Today, see if you would like to choose to show more of yourself in a relationship. See if you would like to embrace the freedom of letting down a part of your image. Is there a relationship in which you would like to relax, value, and reveal yourself just as you are?

Let's begin exploring honesty in a relationship today.

Day 1

Close your eyes and think about what you just read.
What are the first couple of things you notice about
this meditation?

_____

_____

_____

_____

_____

_____

Day 2

Think of the first time you can recall pretending to be
something or someone other than who you really
are.

_____

_____

_____

_____

_____

_____

Day 3

Did a significant caregiver expect you to pretend to have certain thoughts or emotions, and expect you to keep your true thoughts or feelings to yourself?

_____

_____

_____

_____

_____

_____

Day 4

What do you think makes it so difficult for people to tolerate our true feelings at times? (Hint: It doesn't have anything to do with you.)

_____

_____

_____

_____

_____

_____

Day 5

Do you have any relationships where you are comfortable being very honest? What traits in that person or relationship make being honest ok?

_____

_____

_____

_____

_____

_____

Day 6

Can you think of anything valuable to make taking the risks of honesty worth it?

_____

_____

_____

_____

_____

_____

Day 7

Reflect on what you've learned about yourself this week. What have you noticed about honesty in relationships?

_____

_____

_____

_____

_____

_____

Fail with Dignity

Week 4

elieve it or not, it is so important to fail. The life lessons that come through failure are irreplaceable. All people who are very skilled at something have had important failures along the way. Those failures taught them how to better perform that skill. Our culture's obsession with perfection leaves us feeling afraid of failure. There are many resources and messages about "success" – how to get that A, strive for that raise, that bigger house, and that better car. The list of areas to be successful in is long. But what is success, really? Could success be coming to know yourself better, to accept who you are, to accept who others are, making peace with life, learning to adapt to whatever challenges come, and gaining knowledge and information about how the world works? If yes, then imagine how failure might lead to success. Failure teaches us about ourselves. It teaches us what doesn't work for us. Failure gives us information about how not to do it. It gives us feedback about how others and the world work. When we learn by failing, the lesson really sticks. We could read in a book about how to cross-stitch, but that is different than trying it. When we let ourselves try something, it becomes real. Failure makes us learn in three dimensions. Experience is a far better as a teacher than as a punisher.

This week, consider if there is something you want to try failing at. Ponder what would happen if you were to hold your head up high and say, "wow, look what I experienced or learned there! I never would have known that without failure."

Day 1

Close your eyes and think about what you just read. What are the first couple of things you notice about this meditation?

_____

_____

_____

_____

_____

_____

Day 2

Can you remember failing at something important to you?

_____

_____

_____

_____

_____

_____

Day 3

When you have failed at something, what have been the reactions of others toward you?

_____

_____

_____

_____

_____

_____

Day 4

Of the messages you've received about failure, which ones have been motivating you to try the action again or perhaps try something new? Which messages do you want to keep around and which ones do you want to lose?

_____

_____

_____

_____

_____

Day 5

List some messages you would like to be able to give to yourself when you fail at something.

_____

_____

_____

_____

_____

_____

Day 6

Think of a recent or past failure. Tell yourself some of these new messages about that failure.

_____

_____

_____

_____

_____

_____

Day 7

Reflect on what you have learned this week.

_____

_____

_____

_____

_____

_____

Letting go of Expectations

Week 5

When I was young, I wanted to be a lawyer. In my fantasy, my life would be filled with many victories and awards. I would shine and really know that I had made a difference. In our culture, we are often looking for those moments that give us flashy, positive feedback. We look for moments that define who we are and how much we have accomplished. Today, I am reminded that my life is valuable in the "small" differences I make in people's lives. My life matters when I let my best friend know how much she means to me. I matter when I admire my daughter's creation or visit with my son over lunch. Those moments are great. Each of those small stitches or weaves help create the beauty, the comfort, and the smile in the fabric of their lives. What could be so great? Today, I let go of expectations that my wall will be full of awards or that my "accomplishments" need recognition. Today, I rest and relish in the fact that the seemingly small things I do make me very meaningful to some people and make my life very meaningful to me.

Today, we will begin exploring our expectations.

Day 1

Close your eyes and think about what you just read. What are the first couple of things you notice about this meditation?

_____

_____

_____

_____

_____

_____

Day 2

Do you remember, as a child, having any "big" dreams for your future?

_____

_____

_____

_____

_____

_____

Day 3

Did you feel valuable by just being who you were, or were you hoping that achieving your dreams would give you value or importance?

_____

_____

_____

_____

_____

_____

Day 4

Which dreams have you held onto and what motivates you to hang on to them?

_____

_____

_____

_____

_____

_____

Day 5

What dreams have you let go of and why? When did you let go of them?

_____

_____

_____

_____

_____

_____

Day 6

How do you feel about your decisions to hang onto and let go of these dreams/expectations?

_____

_____

_____

_____

_____

_____

Day 7

Reflect on what you have learned about yourself this week.

_____

_____

_____

_____

_____

_____

REALISTIC LONG-TERM RELATIONSHIP VOWS

WEEK 6

I promise to try not to roll my eyes after you tell me for the millionth time that what I did bugged you. I promise to stop, not say anything for a minute, and think before sounding sarcastic or arguing my point. I promise to take responsibility for my own thoughts and feelings. I promise not to ask you to be someone you're not. I promise not to pretend to be someone I'm not. I promise to tell you when I'm having a problem and not let it build up until I'm feeling fed up or hopeless. I promise to ask you to try to be my partner in meeting my needs. I promise to try my best to be your partner in meeting your needs. I promise to love myself. I promise to be happy for you when I see you loving yourself. I promise to continue learning, growing, and adapting. I promise to support your learning and growth. I promise to try to contribute to your healing. And by these things, you will know I love you.

Today, we will look at our relationships realistically.

Day 1

Close your eyes and think about what you just read. What are the first couple of things you notice about this meditation?

_____

_____

_____

_____

_____

_____

Day 2

Were healthy relationships modeled in your childhood?

_____

_____

_____

_____

_____

_____

Day 3

What did you think love was?

_____

_____

_____

_____

_____

_____

Day 4

What have you learned about real relationships?

_____

_____

_____

_____

_____

_____

Day 5

How would you describe love after reflecting on this meditation?

_____

_____

_____

_____

_____

_____

Day 6

In what ways would you like to become more loving?

_____

_____

_____

_____

_____

_____

Day 7

Reflect on what you have learned about yourself this week.

_____

_____

_____

_____

_____

_____

ON GRIEVING

WEEK 7

There is no right way to grieve. No one can tell you which of your buttons grief will push. No one can tell you what loss will mean to you, or of what it will remind you of. Some might smile, some might cry, and some might become anxious. You get to decide. You get to decide when you allow yourself anger, pain, depression, bargaining, guilt, and denial. You get to decide how long it lasts. No one else can tell you the appropriate way to do it. I will only say this about it - if you feel stuck in any one stage, phase, or trigger point, then get help to get unstuck. Grief, like most experiences, is most adaptive when it is flowing through us like water. When it moves freely.

Today, we will feel free to embrace our grief, experience it, honor it, and allow it to cleanse and heal. Only then will we feel truly free to move on.

Day 1

Close your eyes and think about what you just read. What are the first couple of things you notice about this meditation?

_____

_____

_____

_____

_____

_____

Day 2

How did you see grief modeled when you were growing up?

_____

_____

_____

_____

_____

_____

Day 3

Did you personally experience any losses growing up?

_____

_____

_____

_____

_____

_____

Day 4

Were you allowed to have big feelings when you lost something?

_____

_____

_____

_____

_____

_____

Day 5

Which feelings are the most difficult for you to tolerate when you are grieving?

_____

_____

_____

_____

_____

_____

Day 6

What would it mean to you to come to "acceptance" in grief?

_____

_____

_____

_____

_____

_____

Day 7

Reflect on what you learned about yourself this week.

_____

_____

_____

_____

_____

_____

TINY STEPS

WEEK 8

How often do we push ourselves to bite off more than we can chew? Pushing, pushing, pushing. In our culture, there is so much hype about being more than we can be. We idolize those who have broken the mold. When I was a girl, one of the sayings I grew up with was "Good, better, best - let's never rest, until our good is better and our better is best!" Earn more. Have more. Get better now. No room for weakness. But what if that belief system is part of what's causing so many illnesses related to "stress?" What if that mentality is leading us to burn out? How long can any of us keep up at that pace and maintain our sanity, energy, and vitality? It's like running the 50-yard dash for 50 years. Great exercise, but not realistic to think that one could push themselves that hard for that long. What if, instead, a growing number of us decided to re-think where the bar is set. What if we revolted? What if we decided that we want to accept and be comfortable with taking tiny steps in between the big steps? What if we said to ourselves, "I'm ok with appearing unmotivated in exchange for setting realistic goals for myself?" What if we said, "Time for relaxation and relationships is just as important as pushing through?" What if we said, "Today, I deserve to feel accepted as I am taking tiny steps toward my goal?" What could happen if we resist the temptation to push and instead just be?

Today, we will take the time to go at our own pace. We will find joy in embracing tiny steps.

Day 1

Close your eyes and think about what you just read. What are the first couple of things you notice about this meditation?

_____

_____

_____

_____

_____

_____

Day 2

What images did the adults in your life create about achieving goals when you were a child?

_____

_____

_____

_____

_____

_____

Day 3

What are some areas where you are happy that you pushed yourself?

_____

_____

_____

_____

_____

_____

Day 4

What are some areas of your life that you wish you could slow down and accept the way things are, and where you are?

_____

_____

_____

_____

_____

_____

Day 5

What fears within yourself would you have to face to slow down and accept the way things are and where you are? For example, "I'm afraid that I'll become a total failure…"

_____

_____

_____

_____

_____

Day 6

See if you can write down some of the potential benefits of slowing down. See if you can imagine how your body and mind might feel if you were able to slow down and let go a little.

_____

_____

_____

_____

_____

_____

Day 7

Reflect on what you have learned about yourself this week.

_____

_____

_____

_____

_____

_____

Confrontations

Week 9

Confrontation is an art. The next time you need to confront someone, try doing it without much use of the word "you." For example, "This morning when you said that I was acting like a jerk, I thought that my right to be treated with dignity was not being respected, and I felt hurt and angry." Or, for another example, "Yesterday, when I was alone from morning until evening, and waiting to be with my husband, I thought that I was being left alone because I wasn't worthwhile or good enough. And I felt shame and hurt." When something bothers us, it is because there is something in our frame of reference that makes us feel bad about ourselves or about what is happening to us. The way it bothers us comes from our personal history and experiences. Our personal history and experiences don't belong to the other person - they belong to us. It isn't helpful to blame the other person for how we are experiencing the situation. (This doesn't apply to outright abuse.) But, if you are in a viable relationship, then watch how you confront. Take back your power by taking ownership of your experience. Model that behavior. After some time, see if the other person can hear you and act less defensively.

Today, we will strive to be honest with ourselves and to be honest in our communications.

Day 1

Close your eyes and think about what you just read. What are the first couple of things you notice about this meditation?

_____

_____

_____

_____

_____

_____

Day 2

How was communication modeled in your childhood home?

_____

_____

_____

_____

_____

_____

Day 3

What parts of those styles of communication do you re-enact?

_____

_____

_____

_____

_____

_____

Day 4

What do you like about the way you communicate?

_____

_____

_____

_____

_____

_____

Day 5

What would you like to change in the way you communicate?

_____

_____

_____

_____

_____

Day 6

Practice by writing down an example of how you would like to confront someone. It won't make it a habit, but it will start a neural pathway. e.g. When I tried to share my feeling about _____, I didn't think I was listened to. I then got the idea (or memory) that I was unimportant. I felt really sad and mad.

_____

_____

_____

_____

_____

Day 7

Reflect on what you have learned about yourself this week.

_____

_____

_____

_____

_____

_____

More Grieving

Week 10

Sometimes we experience big grief. Sometimes we experience everyday "little" grief. It is so important to know how to make peace with both of those. We may want to block, minimize, dismiss, or distract ourselves from our "little" feelings. Blocking those feelings might feel good for a short time, but then, blocking those feelings will lead to more feelings. The growing mass of feelings may lead to extreme sadness or anxiety. Instead of blocking our feelings, it would be great if we could go right into acknowledgment, validation, and processing. When we work with our feelings, instead of blocking them, we can move through them and move forward. After we process our feelings, we are freed up to experience that joy we so long for in our lives.

Today, we can move toward and embrace grief. We will notice how we judge grief as bad or good and let go of doing that. We will learn to process feelings of grief and move into acceptance and joy.

Day 1

Close your eyes and think about what you just read. What are the first couple of things you notice about this meditation?

_____

_____

_____

_____

_____

_____

Day 2

How was grieving modeled in your childhood?

_____

_____

_____

_____

_____

_____

Day 3

Were you allowed to have feelings over "little" things, or were you told, "it's no big deal, get over it, suck it up?"

_____

_____

_____

_____

_____

_____

Day 4

Can you think of a time when you tried to ignore a "little" thing, and it got bigger or became more significant to you?

_____

_____

_____

_____

_____

_____

Day 5

If you are talking to a friend, would it feel better if they say, "oh I see how you could feel that way"(validation), or "you really should just move on"(invalidation)? Can you validate yourself?

_____

_____

_____

_____

_____

Day 6

Can you let go of judging your feelings as good or bad, and rather say, "I know I am feeling_____, and I'll work with it, and it will pass?

_____

_____

_____

_____

_____

_____

Day 7

Reflect on what you have learned about yourself this week.

_____

_____

_____

_____

_____

_____

Control

Week 11

Control is a basic human desire. I'm not sure why we are born with that desire, because having control is mostly an illusion. We all crave the idea that we can make things happen, make others do something a certain way, or create a desired outcome. Trying to get things to go our way takes up much of our time and energy. What if we could learn to constructively adapt to whatever arises? What if we could just know that, no matter what comes, we could find a way to make ourselves okay? What if we had a "Replenisher 2000" that we could pull out whenever our hearts were broken, whenever we needed to get unstuck from narrow or repetitive thinking, or whenever we needed to creatively problem-solve? Guess what, we do! Our brains can build up an internal "Replenisher 2000." There are many things that can contribute to building this internal "device." Anyone can practice certain behaviors to build a "replenisher." Practice positive self-talk throughout the day, be around generous and satisfied people, and develop spiritual practices. Some of those spiritual practices might include spiritual reading, connection with nature, meditation, spiritual encouragement of yourself or another, and positive visualizations. Doing these things builds up the "replenisher 2000" brain device and relaxes the need to be in control. Instead, we come to believe that "I can handle it. I can face it. Whatever comes, I will find a way through. I will hold my own hand and not let go, and then I will reach out. I will feel safe and not abandoned." And that's all we need to start.

Today, we will learn to hold our own hand to settle our fears. We will let go of the illusion of control and go along for the ride...weeeeeeeeeeeeeeeeeeeeee!

Day 1

Close your eyes and think about what you just read. What are the first couple of things you notice about this meditation?

_____

_____

_____

_____

_____

_____

Day 2

What did you learn about being controlling early in your life?

_____

_____

_____

_____

_____

_____

Day 3

What areas of control have you struggled with in your life?

_____

_____

_____

_____

_____

_____

Day 4

When you gain control of someone else's situation, how long does the feeling of ease last?

_____

_____

_____

_____

_____

_____

Day 5

What would be your biggest fear if you were to stop trying to make something go your way and say, "I guess things are going the way they are supposed to"?

_____

_____

_____

_____

_____

_____

Day 6

Try it and see. Today, pick one manageable item you could stop trying to control and replace the efforts to control with a strategy from the reading.

_____

_____

_____

_____

_____

_____

Day 7

Reflect on what you learned about yourself this week.

_____

_____

_____

_____

_____

_____

HOLDING TWO THINGS

WEEK 12

What a relief it is when we learn that we can hold two opposing thoughts, sensations, or emotional states at the same time. We can be both happy and sad about something. We can feel both excited and scared. We can have a smile and tense shoulders at the same time. We humans are complex beings. Our brains can exist in complex states. A couple of words that help us make sense of this concept are "both" and "part of me." For example, "I feel both happy and scared" or "part of me wants to see them, and part of me doesn't." Sometimes we claim to do things that we "don't want to do." For example, "I really want to lose weight, so I don't know why I keep eating chocolate." The answer is that part of you wants to lose weight, and part of you wants to eat chocolate. If we learn to acknowledge that information, we find out more about that desire to eat chocolate. We can find out how to help that part of us and strike a better balance. If we can say - I want to lose weight "and" I want to eat chocolate, then we aren't denying that part of ourselves. We give it a voice and can help our needs get reasonably met another way.

Today, we choose to notice all our desires and help all parts of us get our needs met.

Day 1

Close your eyes and think about what you just read. What are the first couple of things you notice about this meditation?

_____

_____

_____

_____

_____

_____

Day 2

Do you remember, as a child, sometimes being overwhelmed with feelings? Write about that.

_____

_____

_____

_____

_____

_____

Day 3

Did your parents use black and white thinking, e.g. "you always give up," instead of noticing how well you stuck it out on one thing? (Noticing your growth areas as well as strengths is an example of holding two things.)

_____

_____

_____

_____

_____

Day 4

In your life today, do you notice areas where you have a hard time holding two things? Do you ignore certain desires that a part of you may hold?

_____

_____

_____

_____

_____

Day 5

Identify two ways in which you can do a better job acknowledging two things - e.g. I want to get up early and meditate, and I also want to sleep late.

_____

_____

_____

_____

_____

_____

Day 6

Play around with those desires, and see if you can find a way to make both desires happy - e.g. Every other day I will sleep late, and every other day I will rise earlier to meditate.

_____

_____

_____

_____

_____

_____

Day 7

Reflect on what you have learned about yourself this week.

_____

_____

_____

_____

_____

_____

HOLD ONTO HOPE

WEEK 13

Our knowledge is limited. We can never know everything about ourselves, others, and the universe. When things are bad, never give up hope. We never know when change is just around the corner. Many times in my life, when I was just on the verge of giving up but choosing to hang on, an unexpected change came along. That step brought me closer to my hopes and dreams. There is no way I could have predicted that a turn for the better was coming. I have seen it in many others' lives as well. When we practice the spiritual discipline of enduring, there is a payoff. We can choose to endure with assertiveness, or sometimes make choices to take a different path. Sometimes we have done everything we know to do and haven't found an answer. In some moments, all we have left to do is to cry out. It is often soon after those moments that something shifts.

Today, we will practice holding onto hope, and we will be open to the possibility that change is coming.

Day 1

Close your eyes and think about what you just read. What are the first couple of things you notice about this meditation?

_____

_____

_____

_____

_____

_____

Day 2

Growing up, how was hope modeled or not modeled in your home?

_____

_____

_____

_____

_____

_____

Day 3

When do you struggle with optimism and hope?

_____

_____

_____

_____

_____

_____

Day 4

When are you most hopeful and optimistic?

_____

_____

_____

_____

_____

_____

Day 5

Can you think of a time when a big, unexpected (in a good way) thing happened?

_____

_____

_____

_____

_____

_____

Day 6

What is one area of your life right now where you need to hold onto hope? Write it down and then when the answer comes, come back and write that down - it might be after you've finished this journal.

_____

_____

_____

_____

_____

_____

Day 7

Reflect on what you have learned about yourself this week.

_____

_____

_____

_____

_____

_____

Unprocessed Negative Feelings

Week 14

Unprocessed hurt, pain, anger, resentment, guilt, embarrassment, shame, and fear are like undigested food in the digestive tract. They sit, churn, and start to turn sour. Then, one way or another, those feelings come out. They might emerge like vomit, but they're not staying in there forever. They can't stay in there forever. Undigested emotions are toxic to our emotional, physical, and spiritual systems. Our systems will reject and eject those old emotions. Those feelings need to be acknowledged, grieved, and forgiven. When those feelings are processed, we are freed up to have our focus, energy, and relationships in the present.

Today, we will take inventory of our old feelings. We will do what we need to do to make peace with our past and our feelings about our past.

Day 1

Close your eyes and think about what you just read. What are the first couple of things you notice about this meditation?

_____

_____

_____

_____

_____

_____

Day 2

How did your family, growing up, deal with intense feelings?

_____

_____

_____

_____

_____

_____

Day 3

Do you think there might be any negative events and related feelings from your past that drive your responses today? (Our history drives how we view the world, and sometimes it is rigid, but we can heal and gain more flexibility in our responses.)

_____

_____

_____

_____

_____

Day 4

What are some happy memories that impact you in the present?

_____

_____

_____

_____

_____

_____

Day 5

How to deal with feelings:

*Identify the feelings - guilt, anger, pain, shame, fear, love, joy, passion.

*Notice where you feel the sensations of feelings in your body.

*Validate the feelings - "Everybody has feelings. There is no wrong or right way to have feelings. What you felt/feel is okay."

*Process the feelings - cry, yell, journal, call a friend, talk to your therapist, throw balls.

*Problem-solve – "Is there anything I can do to resolve a situation? Can I take an action that will be helpful? Do I need to do nothing and let the situation pass? Do I need to be assertive"?

*Repeat as necessary.

_____

_____

_____

_____

Day 6

Think of something that has bothered you recently. _

_____

_____

_____

_____

_____

Practice the steps from Day 5.

_____

_____

_____

_____

_____

_____

Day 7

Reflect on what you have learned about yourself this week.

_____

_____

_____

_____

_____

_____

Two Worlds

Week 15

Sometimes I feel utterly caught between two worlds that dwell inside. One says, "rest, be at peace, and enjoy yourself." The other says, "get to work, be productive, and accomplish something." Connecting with those two worlds, at the same time, is an art. Dedicating oneself to the work at hand and the work of the day while, simultaneously, connecting with inner peace, tranquility, and sufficiency, is a spiritual practice. The purpose of work is to provide for us as we live. The purpose of living is to connect with ourselves and our spirituality, and share that with others. Then it doesn't make sense that work would take us so far away from connection.

Today, we will connect with ourselves and our spirituality while we are working. We will recognize that joy and satisfaction are spiritual practices that can be nurtured during both rest and work. We will hold the idea that "rest leads me to rejuvenation, which gives me connection to give back."

Day 1

Close your eyes and think about what you just read.
What are the first couple of things you notice about
this meditation?

_____

_____

_____

_____

_____

_____

Day 2

What were the attitudes toward leisure and work in
your home, growing up?

_____

_____

_____

_____

_____

_____

Day 3

What do you like most about the work you do at home or in a job setting?

_____

_____

_____

_____

_____

_____

Day 4

What is your favorite leisure activity, and what happens in your body when you engage in that activity?

_____

_____

_____

_____

_____

_____

Day 5

Do you find one or the other (leisure or work) more difficult? When do you have a hard time with it?

_____

_____

_____

_____

_____

_____

Day 6

Are there ways in which you could integrate work and enjoyment more - to create better balance?

_____

_____

_____

_____

_____

_____

Day 7

Reflect on what you have learned about yourself this week.

_____

_____

_____

_____

_____

_____

UNINSPIRED

WEEK 16

As an American and a recovering over-achiever, I still love the days where I feel inspired. But what about all the days I feel uninspired? What about all the humdrum, dull days in between the fun, motivating, something to write home about days? Do those count for anything? Is it ok to have dull days? Do I still matter when I'm not producing something awe-inspiring, saving the world, or creating a brand-new product or thought? Can those hum drum days have value and meaning for my life? Well, I can imagine what life would be like without them. Without them, I would never slow down, never take time to be contemplative, or face the demons that lurk in the shadows. I'm not sure there would be any room for humility, compassion for human suffering, or connecting with others from need. I'm not sure there would be room for allowing myself to be loved in my inglorious state, rather than just when I'm feeling glorious.

Today, we will find those internal, quiet, stone-unturned places. We will love and be loved as a result. We will be loved just as we are.

Day 1

Close your eyes and think about what you just read.
What are the first couple of things you notice about
this meditation?

_____

_____

_____

_____

_____

_____

Day 2

Growing up, did your family take time to sit and do
nothing?

_____

_____

_____

_____

_____

_____

Day 3

What is it like for you when you are between projects, goals, or just not connecting with them?

_____

_____

_____

_____

_____

_____

Day 4

Do you use busyness to distract yourself from uncomfortable thoughts or feelings?

_____

_____

_____

_____

_____

_____

Day 5

Envision using downtime as an opportunity to practice full acceptance of yourself, right where you are in that moment. For example, "I make peace with my unrest. I embrace my lack of direction. I trust that this discomfort will be a good friend to me."

_____

_____

_____

_____

_____

Day 6

Create a statement of gratitude for those types of days. For example, "I am grateful for a change of pace inside myself."

_____

_____

_____

_____

_____

_____

Day 7

Reflect on what you have learned about yourself this week.

_____

_____

_____

_____

_____

_____

DO FOR YOURSELF

WEEK 17

The title of this week's reading sounds selfish, doesn't it? What's with our culture? We have these strict rules about not being selfish, but then we become aware of selfishness leaking out all over the place. What's wrong with admitting that one aspect of our humanness is selfishness? Where do we draw the line on our selfishness? There's an idea that I like to call "healthy selfish" vs "unhealthy selfish." Healthy selfish is taking care of myself in a way that does not take away from or trample on the right of others to take care of themselves. Unhealthy selfish seeks to meet my own needs at the cost of another. I think "healthy selfish" is the same thing as "good self-care." But, there is still a strange dichotomy that we are either identified as a selfish or a selfless person. The labels "selfish" or "selfless" get in the way of freedom and flexibility to practice self-care. What if we could just put away the extremes for a little while? What if we could see that we can balance caring for ourselves with caring for others?

I will not look to others to do for me what I would like to do for myself. And I will care for myself in a way that is not disrespecting or demeaning of anyone else. I will care for myself in a way that will leave me full and satisfied. Then I will pass on goodness to others.

Today, we will practice healthy selfishness.

Day 1

Close your eyes and think about what you just read. What are the first couple of things you notice about this meditation?

_____

_____

_____

_____

_____

_____

Day 2

What were the messages in your childhood home regarding selfishness?

_____

_____

_____

_____

_____

_____

Day 3

Was there any hypocrisy around selfishness?

_____

_____

_____

_____

_____

_____

Day 4

Do you judge yourself and/or others for being selfish?

_____

_____

_____

_____

_____

_____

Day 5

Imagine what it would feel like for you to embrace "healthy selfish," e.g. honoring yourself with 10 minutes of breathing exercises every day, honoring yourself with a daily exercise practice, meditating 10 minutes a day, setting aside 20 minutes for pleasure reading, a 20-minute hot bath...

_____

_____

_____

_____

_____

Day 6

Identify a healthy, selfish behavior you can do today. Set your intention to it and guard that time religiously. Then note how you feel afterward.

_____

_____

_____

_____

_____

Day 7

Reflect on what you have learned about yourself this week.

_____

_____

_____

_____

_____

_____

FIRM EDGES, FLEXIBLE CENTER

WEEK 18

Our values, beliefs, experiences, and personalities give us the structure to make choices and decisions every day. Inside of that structure, the fluidity and ease of a flowing spirit give us the ability to adapt, weather, and grow with each of life's challenges. It's like the flexible water of a creek, flowing between the structured edges and bottom of the creek bank. It bends and finds a way to keep moving. The water is like our life force. If it gets dammed up, it might overflow. If it dries up, the creek life goes with it. Resistances creates little pools that just spin round and round. The hard banks and bottom can and will be amended, but usually slowly and with time. The healthiest creeks flow openly and freely. They invite a variety of life forms to be supported and nurtured by them. They are the hub of rich biodiversity. Like creeks, our inner resources of acceptance, care, love, adaptability, and flexibility invite a rich interrelatedness with those around us.

Today, we will begin moving forward from a place of accepting exactly who we are with a moment to moment willingness for becoming who we will be.

Day 1

Close your eyes and think about what you just read. What are the first couple of things you notice about this meditation?

_____

_____

_____

_____

_____

_____

Day 2

Growing up, did you have rigid roles that you had to play, or were you allowed to be spontaneous and flexible?

_____

_____

_____

_____

_____

_____

Day 3

Today, what are some of your internal roadblocks, around which you have to learn to flow?

_____

_____

_____

_____

_____

_____

Day 4

What are some of those "little pools" that make you feel like you spin around and around without going anywhere?

_____

_____

_____

_____

_____

_____

Day 5

When are times you feel you "flow freely?" What things, people, practices invite your acceptance, love, care, adaptability, and flexibility?

_____

_____

_____

_____

_____

_____

Day 6

Make a statement of acceptance to practice daily - e.g. I accept myself wholly and unconditionally today and each day.

_____

_____

_____

_____

_____

_____

Day 7

Reflect on what you have learned about yourself this week.

_____

_____

_____

_____

_____

_____

DEATH

WEEK 19

Death is an important part of the lifecycle. It is natural. Death makes us feel things we can often avoid in our everyday lives. Death may make us feel very sad and mad and empty. It makes us evaluate our past and our future. Death is real and raw, and it makes us face it, whether we want to or not. We have to believe that it serves a purpose that is common to all humans. And all humans must, at one point or another, come into contact with death. When we are faced with death, what can we do to support one another? We cannot take away the feelings that death brings, but we can stand alongside someone as they face it. We can be patient about their grieving. We can overcome our own avoidances and reach out. We can give a friendly smile or shed an empathetic tear. We can listen.

Today, we will respectfully reach out and support those who have been touched by death. We will honor their experience as normal and natural. We will have the courage to face their loss with them.

Day 1

Close your eyes and think about what you just read. What are the first couple of things you notice about this meditation?

_____

_____

_____

_____

_____

_____

Day 2

When were you first impacted by death?

_____

_____

_____

_____

_____

_____

Day 3

What was that experience like for you - was it positive, filled with love? Were you on your own with it? Did people's fear scare you? Did you feel supported and attended to in your experience?

_____

_____

_____

_____

_____

Day 4

What are your beliefs about death now? What emotions do you experience now when you think of someone dying?

_____

_____

_____

_____

_____

_____

Day 5

Are there some people in your life whom you would trust to support you in a loss? Are there others you would not? What about those you would trust makes you have that trust in them?

_____

_____

_____

_____

_____

Day 6

Can others reach out to you for support - it's ok whether they can or can't. Just notice, without judgment, whether or not you feel capable in this area.

_____

_____

_____

_____

_____

Day 7

Reflect on what you have learned about yourself this week.

_____

_____

_____

_____

_____

_____

POWER OUT

WEEK 20

I wonder if it is actually very good for us to have the power go out once in a while? You might be so present in the moment that you make wax sculptures from melted candle wax. The noises of the city get quiet. Things change. Only the most important things really seem important anymore. You wonder if there is enough power to keep the hospital going. You think about whether you have clean drinking water. How will I heat up food? Just the basics. All the other "needs" of life get fuzzy. Only the true needs for survival are in sharp focus. I wonder if this somehow helps reset us for a little while. Having the power out helps us remember all those other things we worry so much about are not true emergencies. We remember that we could get by with a more minimalistic sense of necessity. Of course, it is ok to enjoy things that aren't necessary! But we run into problems when we deem unnecessary things to be necessary. Our thinking and vision become distorted and cloudy.

Today, we will pretend that the power is out for a little while. We will take a few minutes to focus on the difference between "need" and need. We will reset our "need" o meter and relax.

Day 1

Close your eyes and think about what you just read. What are the first couple of things you notice about this meditation?

_____

_____

_____

_____

_____

_____

Day 2

When you think of childhood "needs," what do you remember?

_____

_____

_____

_____

_____

_____

Day 3

When you notice your needs, how do you think and feel about them?

_____

_____

_____

_____

_____

_____

Day 4

How do you define "need?"

_____

_____

_____

_____

_____

_____

Day 5

Can you tease out some differences between needs and wants?

_____

_____

_____

_____

_____

_____

Day 6

List some of your needs - physical, spiritual, emotional, social.

_____

_____

_____

_____

_____

_____

Day 7

Reflect on what you have learned about yourself this week.

_____

_____

_____

_____

_____

_____

WAITING

WEEK 21

I love the part in "Oh, The Places You'll Go" where the author pens about "the waiting place." I wonder how much of our lives are spent waiting? I wonder whether there is any spiritual discipline to waiting? What could we learn from waiting? I think our growth is partially about how we wait. We are not really present to what this moment could offer if we can only wait with an impatient, foot-tapping pressure about what we need to be doing elsewhere. What if, instead, we choose to wait with gratitude. What if waiting right now is going to put us at just the right time and place, during our day for a little miracle to unfold? What if we can use this waiting as a time to breathe and reflect? What if this waiting is the quiet before a noisy time? Could we avail ourselves of the time to store up some energy? Who are we to say what is the best timing of things in the universe? We can't get around having to wait.

Today, we will use our waiting times to stop, reflect, journal, and breathe. We will be fully prepared and present for what this and the next moment holds.

Day 1

Close your eyes and think about what you just read. What are the first couple of things you notice about this meditation?

_____

_____

_____

_____

_____

_____

Day 2

Who was the most patient person in your life growing up?

_____

_____

_____

_____

_____

_____

Day 3

What does it feel like when you are impatient?

_____

_____

_____

_____

_____

_____

Day 4

Do you trust that things unfold at just the right times in your life?

_____

_____

_____

_____

_____

_____

Day 5

What scares you about waiting?

_____

_____

_____

_____

_____

_____

Day 6

Imagine a situation where you are waiting. While imagining that situation, breathe and let your body relax. Try it again.

_____

_____

_____

_____

_____

_____

Day 7

Reflect on what you learned about yourself this week.

_____

_____

_____

_____

_____

_____

Never Say "Never"

Week 22

never think that someone you know or love won't or can't change. I'm not saying, "put your life on hold in hopes that it will happen." If you are dealing with a difficult behavior of another's, you may need to move on. You will certainly need to find strategies to cope and to make yourself okay. But never say "never" because you just don't know. The universe is at work in all of us to produce growth and healing. The universe is at work to produce stronger, deeper, more generous and loving humans. We may not see evidence of that at every moment, but we don't have a crystal ball. We don't know what forces are at work in another's life to make them better. There are so many times when I gave up and let go of something I wanted for another, and then the transformation came and surprised me. Consider this: give up on needing to be in control, let go and watch.

Today, we will let go and say, "yep, it's not up to us when, but that change could happen."

Day 1

Close your eyes and think about what you just read. What are the first couple of things you notice about this meditation?

_____

_____

_____

_____

_____

Day 2

Was there anyone in your family who was prone to becoming emotionally stuck, or held grudges? Were people able to let go, or did they hold onto hurts as if they were trophies?

_____

_____

_____

_____

_____

_____

Day 3

How might saying "she'll never change" be, in a way, protective to oneself?

_____

_____

_____

_____

_____

_____

Day 4

What are the benefits and what are the costs of that protection? (e.g. benefit - I don't get disappointed, cost - I feel resentful.)

_____

_____

_____

_____

_____

_____

Day 5

What if you could take your focus off that thing about the other person and refocus on a way to care for yourself if that thing happens?

_____

_____

_____

_____

_____

_____

Day 6

What if you could believe that all change comes at just the intended moment?

_____

_____

_____

_____

_____

_____

Day 7

Reflect on what you have learned about yourself this
week.

_____

_____

_____

_____

_____

_____

THE IMPORTANCE OF REJECTION

WEEK 23

One of the most painful experiences is the sting of rejection. Rejection can start the wheels spinning - "Am I good enough? Is there something wrong with me? Have I done something wrong? Am I worthless?" Those questions are important ones for us to recognize and face. When those questions come, it would be good if we could welcome them as opportunities to re-attest to our value and worth. Value and worth are things we are born with, but sometimes can forget that we have. Sometimes we imagine value and worth as something we earn, or as flexible points, depending on how we have performed. When we are questioning our value and worth, we might get those sensations of a spinning head, shortness of breath, and a difficulty in concentrating. And then... we can become aware that this is an opportunity to practice calming, comforting, and reassuring ourselves. We might say, "My inherent value and worth never change. As a human, I am entitled to the basic rights of value and worth. I am no more or less valuable than any other human." This is an opportunity to practice knowing who we are with an unwillingness to turn away from or abandon ourselves. Struggling with rejection is also an opportunity we can draw from when connecting with others. Everyone has had the experience of feeling rejected. What makes a difference is the ability to create connection with ourselves or another from that "negative" event.

Today, when we notice rejection, we will use it as an opportunity to reach for connection with ourselves or another.

Day 1

Close your eyes and think about what you just read. What are the first couple of things you notice about this meditation?

_____

_____

_____

_____

_____

_____

Day 2

How was handling rejection modeled in your home? What did your family believe about how to manage rejection?

_____

_____

_____

_____

_____

_____

Day 3

Think of a time you experienced rejection. How did you handle that? Did you find yourself having negative thoughts about that?

_____

_____

_____

_____

_____

Day 4

Can you imagine how to calm or comfort yourself when you feel rejected - e.g. "I love and value myself unconditionally. I will hold onto my strengths and values, even in the face of rejection. I will trust that others will heal of the need to reject me"? Write your own statement.

_____

_____

_____

_____

_____

Day 5

Imagine a friend or loved one is suffering the sting of rejection - what might you say to comfort them?

_____

_____

_____

_____

_____

_____

Day 6

How might a rejection help you grow and become more mature?

_____

_____

_____

_____

_____

_____

Day 7

Reflect on what you have learned about yourself this week.

_____

_____

_____

_____

_____

_____

THE PERFECT RELATIONSHIP

WEEK 24

What makes the perfect relationship? For some, it is loud fighting. For some, it is no fighting. Some relationships need a lot of excitement. Some people are happy sitting around together. For some, it is being similar. For others, it is being different. Some value children and some don't want to have kids. Some people fit well when they get married young, some when they're old, and some in between. So consider all the possible factors. Then consider this: the perfect relationship is when two flawed humans admit their weaknesses and struggles, apologize for those shortcomings, and live each day with the intention of being open to and seeking growth and healing. If you have found that in someone - they are perfect for you.

Today, we will continue to seek growth and healing, and we will look for that in others.

Day 1

Close your eyes and think about what you just read. What are the first couple of things you notice about this meditation?

_____

_____

_____

_____

_____

_____

Day 2

What kind of relationship did your parents or caregivers have?

_____

_____

_____

_____

_____

_____

Day 3

What kinds of adult relationship did you see modeled, in general?

_____

_____

_____

_____

_____

_____

Day 4

What memories, of adults relating, do you like? What memories are bothersome?

_____

_____

_____

_____

_____

_____

Day 5

Do you ever have trouble admitting your mistakes? Why do you think that is - does it feel as if there is a perceived cost of doing that? Or perhaps, someone close to you has trouble - what do you think the cost is to them?

_____

_____

_____

_____

_____

Day 6

Think of one way in which you would like to grow and/or heal with regard to your relationships.

_____

_____

_____

_____

_____

_____

Day 7

Reflect on what you have learned about yourself this week.

_____

_____

_____

_____

_____

_____

ONE WHOLE

WEEK 25

Our minds (beliefs, memories, and experiences), bodies, thoughts, and emotions are inextricably connected. When we lose contact with our own body, our minds spin and race. We may feel as though we are floating, rather than having solid contact with the earth beneath us. When we go with only what we are sensing in our bodies, we aren't able to utilize our wisdom to know what to do next. When our emotions are running the show, we will experience peaks and valleys in mood, and our relationships will become chaotic. There is no one of these parts of us that is better than any other. It is the connection of all of these parts that gives rise to a reliable, stable, rich, and rewarding human experience. And it is the connecting of these parts that bear forth our spirituality and ability to bestow a positive footprint beneath us and with those around us.

Today, we will find ways to pay attention to each part of us. Whether it be through meditation, deep breathing, play, journaling, giving a smile, correcting our flawed thinking, or practicing warmly accepting our emotions –we will be open to nurturing a connection with our entire selves.

Day 1

Close your eyes and think about what you just read. What are the first couple of things you notice about this meditation?

_____

_____

_____

_____

_____

_____

Day 2

Have you ever observed behaviors, in others, that would make you think they might not be functioning as a whole?

_____

_____

_____

_____

_____

_____

Day 3

Did your parents have balance, or do you remember areas where they were out of balance?

_____

_____

_____

_____

_____

_____

Day 4

When are the times you feel least whole - like you just can't get all of you working together?

_____

_____

_____

_____

_____

_____

Day 5

When are the times you feel most whole - like you just handled something amazingly well or you were feeling generous or really relaxed or satisfied?

_____

_____

_____

_____

_____

_____

Day 6

What activities or practices help you feel whole? Practice those today. See if you are open to making them regular practices.

_____

_____

_____

_____

_____

_____

Day 7

Reflect on what you learned about yourself this week.

_____

_____

_____

_____

_____

_____

Every Moment

Week 26

Every moment is an opportunity. We don't choose how we feel about something. But we can choose how we respond to how we feel. First, it is a good idea to notice and name how we feel. Is it anger, shame, pain, guilt, or fear? Next, it helps to take a breath and accept how we feel. After that, we can journal, call a friend, punch the bed, go for a walk, pray, or any other non- harmful action that helps us experience the feelings as fluid and fleeting rather than stuck and consuming. Then we can take note whether we have been able to let a little bit of the feeling go. Have we been able to come to some peace? If we are still activated, then we can go through the process again. Why is it helpful to do these steps? Because every moment is an opportunity to make peace with life instead of fighting it. Every moment is an opportunity to make peace within ourselves and with others; to deepen within ourselves and move more fully into love and compassion. These qualities make our relationships rich and deep, and our lives more satisfying. These qualities make life worth living.

Today, we will notice whether we can experience difficult emotions as opportunities to connect with ourselves and others. We will notice that we can have some influence on how we respond to our feelings.

Day 1

Close your eyes and think about what you just read. What are the first couple of things you notice about this meditation?

_____

_____

_____

_____

_____

_____

Day 2

How did people react to feelings as you were growing up? Were there some feelings that were considered inappropriate or off limits?

_____

_____

_____

_____

_____

_____

Day 3

What feelings are the most difficult for you to accept or express?

_____

_____

_____

_____

_____

_____

Day 4

When you are needing to express feelings, what methods of doing so work for you? Which methods seem non-productive?

_____

_____

_____

_____

_____

_____

Day 5

Each feeling comes with a gift. All feelings are useful. Can you imagine what it would be like to be at peace with your feelings and not fight or judge any of them?

_____

_____

_____

_____

_____

Day 6

Pick a feeling (one you struggle with) to notice and track for two days. Can you welcome it when it comes? Can you breathe into it and let it give you a gift?

_____

_____

_____

_____

_____

Day 7

Reflect on what you have learned about yourself this week.

_____

_____

_____

_____

_____

_____

GOOD AND BAD

WEEK 27

wonder if I could encourage us to use the words "good" and "bad" sparingly - especially when it comes to judgments about ourselves or others? For instance, rather than thinking "I made a good decision," we might choose to think "I made a decision that had a certain outcome. I liked this part of how it turned out." Likewise, rather than choosing to judge a decision as "bad," we might choose to think "I don't like how that turned out. These consequences have been really painful. I am hurting as a result of that decision I made." Sometimes, even when we are hurting as a result of a decision, the decision will still have some benefits to it. Weigh how much positive vs negative has come from the decision, and then think about what you can learn and how you can grow from it. This truth is, there are a handful of things in life that are unequivocally "good" or "bad." **The rest is pure learning.** Be careful about judging another person as "bad." It could be that, one day, we find ourselves in a similar situation, making a similar decision. It is okay to notice and recognize the traits we find difficult in another person. And others may notice and do the same with us.

Today, instead of judging choices and people as "good" or "bad," I will be descriptive about my emotional response to a decision or another person.

Day 1

Close your eyes and think about what you just read. What are the first couple of things you notice about this meditation?

_____

_____

_____

_____

_____

Day 2

It is normal development for children to view the world as "good" and "bad." Were there adults in your life who continued using those categories past childhood?

_____

_____

_____

_____

_____

Day 3

Think of a few things that you think are universally bad or good - e.g., killing another person without cause, or helping someone in need when it is safe to do so.

_____

_____

_____

_____

_____

Day 4

Have you ever labeled things, people, situations as good or bad and then later changed your mind about them?

_____

_____

_____

_____

_____

_____

Day 5

Are there people, things, decisions in your life now that might benefit from less good or bad thinking and more descriptive thinking, e.g. yesterday when I decided to _____, I liked the way _____ turned out/didn't turn out. (Or) Mrs. _____ really rubs me the wrong way when she _____, and I like it when she _____.

_____

_____

_____

_____

Day 6

Label the feelings you have as a result of an important decision - sad, angry, lonely, joyful, etc. Comfort and nurture yourself for having those feelings.

_____

_____

_____

_____

Day 7

Reflect on what you have learned about yourself this week.

_____

_____

_____

_____

_____

_____

Saying Goodbye

Week 28

There are probably times when saying "goodbye" feels like an easy thing, but there are many times when it feels very difficult. We get used to having someone here. We get used to their mannerisms, their laughs, their fears, and the way they move through life. They become comfortable and familiar. We make a place in our heart and mind for them. And when we say "goodbye," what do we do with that place? Do we leave it empty, try to fill it with something else, or try to pretend it doesn't exist? Perhaps, we could find a way to keep it full with our memories with them. Perhaps, we could reminisce about the times we danced together, laughed together, told jokes together, and cried together. We can think about how they came into our lives at a time when we really needed them to be who they were for us. Perhaps, we could find new ways to connect with them - a text, a prayer, or an e-mail. It won't be the same, but those things can help. We can also choose to send them, with a full heart, knowing that other people; new people, will come to need them in the same way that we have.

Today, we will learn to say "goodbye" in a way that holds their memory and their place in our hearts, while also letting go in a way that frees them to move on.

Day 1

Close your eyes and think about what you just read. What are the first couple of things you notice about this meditation?

_____

_____

_____

_____

_____

_____

Day 2

Loss is a regular part of life. This isn't about death but about people moving away from each other. Growing up, how did people in your family handle such losses?

_____

_____

_____

_____

_____

_____

Day 3

What is the most difficult part of saying goodbye? What feelings does that bring up?

_____

_____

_____

_____

_____

_____

Day 4

What are your go-to methods for handling loss? (crying, eating, exercising, talking, writing, etc.) What strategies do you like?

_____

_____

_____

_____

_____

_____

Day 5

What strategies don't work for you? Why? Are there some strategies you would like to put in their place?

_____

_____

_____

_____

_____

Day 6

Think of some losses - send some positive thoughts toward them - e.g. to that manager who didn't hire me - I hope the person who got that job is really benefiting from it. To the friends who moved away - I hope you are loving your new town and enjoying what it has to offer, etc.

_____

_____

_____

_____

_____

Day 7

Reflect on what you have learned about yourself this week.

_____

_____

_____

_____

_____

_____

Speaking Up

Week 29

Having a voice and speaking up are very important parts of close relationships. It is also important for us to be realistic about the goals and possible outcomes of our speaking up. We get it in our minds to speak up "so that" he will change this, "so that" she will do that differently. The only "so that" guarantee we have is "so that" we will be better known, and that those parts of us who have felt devalued, ignored, or otherwise unworthy will be restored to a state of voice and worthiness. As children, we hoped it was our parents' voice who affirmed our worth and value as people. As adults, it is our own voice that affirms our worth and value as people. We never have the guarantee that speaking up will get us what we want, but it does change us from the inside out. It empowers us to advocate for ourselves. It tells those small-feeling parts of us that it is okay to be who we are. Speaking up tells us that we have a right to take up space on this earth. And it allows those who are close to us to know the truth about who we are. Yes - we risk being rejected. We risk having people say they can't love us for who we are. That is livable. Rejecting ourselves and refusing to love ourselves for who we are is not livable. We can heal from rejection by another, but we cannot move forward while actively rejecting ourselves.

Today, we will tune in to our inner voice and practice speaking up "so that" we will value ourselves and "so that" people who are close to us will know who we are.

Day 1

Close your eyes and think about what you just read. What are the first couple of things you notice about this meditation?

_____

_____

_____

_____

_____

_____

Day 2

In your childhood, was speaking up a tool for manipulation, or was it used as a tool for sharing? Maybe different people modeled it differently?

_____

_____

_____

_____

_____

_____

Day 3

Is there anyone in your life now, that you really like the way they share things. They can share, and you still feel valued in the face of what they are sharing?

_____

_____

_____

_____

_____

_____

Day 4

What sorts of things do you have difficulty sharing with people who are close to you?

_____

_____

_____

_____

_____

_____

Day 5

What would you have to believe to make sharing easier? - e.g. what I have to say is important, I am strong, I will remove myself from punishment (by others or myself) if I share openly, I am safe.

_____

_____

_____

_____

_____

Day 6

Do an experiment today - get really curious about what it would be like to share something that you have been afraid to share - share it and notice how you react, how the other person reacts. Just take note of it for reflection.

_____

_____

_____

_____

_____

Day 7

What have you learned about yourself this week?

_____

_____

_____

_____

_____

_____

JUST BREATHE

WEEK 30

In "Comfortable With Uncertainty," Pema Chodron talks about the power of breathing in and breathing out. So often; in our busy, rush, rush, and fear driven society, we move about while forgetting to breathe. It sounds so easy - just breathe (deeply). But we don't. Instead, we hold our breath or participate in shallow breathing. There is a good, evolutionary purpose for shallow breathing and breath holding. Shallow breathing is for when trying to escape a physically dangerous situation. The blood rushes, the adrenal glands pump adrenaline, and the body gets flooded with cortisol. The brain focuses down to only the most critical, life-saving decisions. This is great when being chased by a saber-toothed tiger or when reacting to a near car accident. "Thank you, body." This is not great while trying to negotiate the everyday, more commonplace, choices and life-decisions that require calm and higher thinking. It is not good for our bodies to live in a perpetual state of readiness. We can get adrenal fatigue and exhaustion. On the contrary, deep breathing promotes relaxation, higher reasoning, and transcendence. Learning to breathe deeply can be accomplished by lying on your back, placing a book on your abdomen, and breathing so deeply that you make the book move up and down. Then, as you breathe in - breathe into those places in your body that may be suffering or uncomfortable. Finally, as you exhale, say a word that you want to expand within yourself - e.g. "love, compassion, strength, hope, peace, happy" and move toward transcendence. Make a practice of breathing.

Today, we will set a reminder to encourage ourselves to practice at least one daily, deep breath. We will make deep breathing a regular part of our lives.

Day 1

Close your eyes and think about what you just read. What are the first couple of things you notice about this meditation?

_____

_____

_____

_____

_____

_____

Day 2

Were there any specific times in your life when you think you learned to hold or shallow your breath?

_____

_____

_____

_____

_____

_____

Day 3

Today, observe and pay attention to your breathing. Without judgment, just notice times when you might be breathing deeply and notice times when you might be breathing shallowly or holding your breath.

_____

_____

_____

_____

_____

_____

Day 4

What are you observing about your breath?

_____

_____

_____

_____

_____

_____

Day 5

Set an intention for breathing - e.g. I will breathe deeply once a day for 7 days, I will make a daily reminder to check my breathing at 12:00, I will practice breathing with the book twice a week, I will find a breathing app for my phone to help me practice, I will attend yoga, etc.

_____

_____

_____

_____

_____

Day 6

What are the difficult or easy parts of a deep breathing practice?

_____

_____

_____

_____

_____

Day 7

Reflect on what you have learned about yourself this week.

_____

_____

_____

_____

_____

_____

LIFE TEACHERS

WEEK 31

This reading is about teachers, but not in the traditional sense of the word. This is not about someone who goes to college and gets a teaching credential. This is about the teacher in all of us. For we are all one another's teachers. We have something to learn from everyone with whom we come into contact, every day. Those around us teach us about ourselves. When we react to something in someone else, that reminds us to notice ourselves. What was it we didn't like about that, and why? Have we ever noticed that same trait in ourselves, and do we reject that trait in ourselves, or can we be still and notice ourselves, without judgment? Clearly, people have differences and value different things. And clearly, we don't all behave the same way. So how could we learn from someone with whom we have very little in common? The truth is; as humans, we have a lot in common. We all want to be accepted. We all want to know and feel love. We all have a survival instinct. We all want to feel some sense of predictability and control. So, what could I learn from the thief who burgled my office last year? Maybe, I learn sometimes we humans are suffering and feel helpless and powerless to ease that suffering or find another path. Then we build a wall toward others and aren't able to empathize with the suffering we cause the other person. When we are treated poorly, it helps if we can notice our own suffering and accept it. It then helps to imagine the suffering that the other person must be feeling or have endured. We wonder what we can learn from it.

We can also learn from being treated well. It makes us feel good and reminds us of the good in ourselves and others. When someone takes the time to smile, hold a door, or give a compliment, we may feel valued. And we can pass that feeling on to another.

Today, we will see all humans around us as our teachers, and we will open ourselves to learning and growing from every contact we have with another person.

Day 1

Close your eyes and think about what you just read. What are the first couple of things you notice about this meditation?

_____

_____

_____

_____

_____

_____

Day 2

Think about the impact the first important people in your life had on you. Did they teach you that it is ok for you and others to make mistakes and learn?

_____

_____

_____

_____

_____

_____

Day 3

Are there people who have made a "bad" situation for you? Did you learn anything from that situation?

_____

_____

_____

_____

_____

_____

Day 4

Who have been some of your favorite teachers (remember: friends, family, mentors, etc.) in your life?

_____

_____

_____

_____

_____

_____

Day 5

Who do you think has learned from you? To whom have you been a teacher?

_____

_____

_____

_____

_____

_____

Day 6

Come up with an encouraging phrase for when you are learning a hard lesson from a difficult teacher. E.g. - I am having a really hard time with _____, and they are helping me learn to...

_____

_____

_____

_____

_____

_____

Day 7

Reflect on what you have learned about yourself this week.

_____

_____

_____

_____

_____

_____

THE SNUCKLE

WEEK 32

I just finished a biography about Dr. Seuss, and this is a dedication to Theodore Seuss Geisel. We all have a snuckle to cherish and share. Some snuckles are brown, some orange, and some with flair. "My snuckle belongs to me," we say. And it does, it does! Enjoy it with much fun and with glee. Your snuckle has color and texture and bounce. Your snuckle is one that is not easily snuffed out. Some folks will try to temper your snuckle. They'll cover and hide it and tell you it's wrong. They seem they don't want your snuckle along. But there is no one in the world with a snuckle like you. Your snuckle is the one and only like you. So, whether your snuckle is big, red, or purple, or whether your snuckle is square with a nurple, don't ever try to have someone else's snuckle. No, it's not for you! The world needs YOUR snuckle. You have something to do. Your snuckle is needed by all. Your snuckle is a gift. It is your call. So, love your snuckle, and many will love it too. And you'll be doing your part of the snuckle snugoo - that keeps us all happy and dappy and loved. It keeps us going and marching in tune. It keeps us marching all the way through gloomy lagoon. I need your snuckle, and you need mine. We'll share today. And we'll all be just fine!

Today, we will appreciate ourselves for EXACTLY who we are.

Day 1

Close your eyes and think about what you just read. What are the first couple of things you notice about this meditation?

_____

_____

_____

_____

_____

_____

Day 2

Growing up, were people viewed through the lens of their faults, or were people viewed for their strengths and value they bring?

_____

_____

_____

_____

_____

_____

Day 3

What are your favorite things about yourself? What do you value about yourself?

_____

_____

_____

_____

_____

_____

Day 4

In what ways are you hard on yourself? Where do you get judgmental and look through the lens of faults?

_____

_____

_____

_____

_____

_____

Day 5

Name an area in which you would like to learn to be more kind and gentle with others?

_____

_____

_____

_____

_____

_____

Day 6

Name an area in which you would like to be more kind and gentle with yourself? Make a gentle statement to say to yourself when you do the thing that bothers you.

_____

_____

_____

_____

_____

_____

Day 7

Reflect on what you learned about yourself this week.

_____

_____

_____

_____

_____

_____

BE THE BUTTERFLY

WEEK 33

ost of us have heard the metaphor likening a caterpillar turning into a butterfly to human transformation. But I learned a little something more today about that process, that adds so much to the metaphor. When a caterpillar is still developing in its egg (before it ever even becomes a fully developed caterpillar), it grows "imaginal discs" (groups of highly developed cells) - one for each of the body parts it will need to become an adult butterfly. Later, when it digests itself in its cocoon, those imaginal discs do not get digested. These imaginal discs fuel the process of the butterfly's development and emergence. This is exactly how we humans are. When we are developing, we come into the world with "imaginal discs" - traits, characteristics, personalities, genetics, or whatever else you want to call them. Those cells (parts of us) wait for the right circumstances, environment, and encouragement to turn us into moldable form. Then these "imaginal" parts of us can do their jobs. It is then that those traits can fuel our transformational process and be fully revealed and emergent. I love that they are called "imaginal." I love that we can dream big about who we are. I love that, in the course of our lives, we can go from looking and feeling one way to something completely transformed. I have the privilege of seeing transformation every day. I love that life looks at us and imagines all of who we can be. Neuroscience research tells us that when we imagine something such as a waterfall or ocean wave, the same neurons get activated that would get activated if we were actually standing in front of that waterfall or ocean wave.

Today, we will take some time to dream our "imaginal" selves. We will envision ourselves in the biggest, most expansive ways possible. We will imagine ourselves as we are to become. And we will be the butterflies.

Day 1

Close your eyes and think about what you just read. What are the first couple of things you notice about this meditation?

_____

_____

_____

_____

_____

_____

Day 2

When you were little, did you have any imaginings about what you would do or what your life would look like when you grew up?

_____

_____

_____

_____

_____

_____

Day 3

What parts of your imaginings have you let go of? What parts have you hung onto?

_____

_____

_____

_____

_____

_____

Day 4

From where you are now, imagine the ways in which you would like to grow and become more you, more whole.

_____

_____

_____

_____

_____

_____

Day 5

This is important. Spend some more time imagining your most evolved self. Actually see and feel how it would be to be that version of you.

_____

_____

_____

_____

_____

_____

Day 6

Give your vision of you a name. Practice saying that name and bringing this vision to mind.

_____

_____

_____

_____

_____

_____

Day 7

Reflect on what you have learned about yourself this week.

_____

_____

_____

_____

_____

_____

WHOLE PERSON

WEEK 34

We are each a whole person. We cannot express the fullness of who we are while, at the same time, denying a part of ourselves. Sometimes we learn to hide parts of who we are. We learn to put away thoughts, memories, hopes, and desires with the goal of making our lives less painful, scary, shameful, or guilty. And that works, for a while. For a while, we can pretend that something didn't happen. For a while, we can deny the trait in ourselves that causes us negative feelings. For a while we can go on skating around these treacherous places. But then one day, they catch up with us. We notice that the dam gets leaky. We notice sudden, intrusive thoughts or urges. We have to decide what to do with them. Do we add a new layer in trying to stash them away? Do we go to even greater lengths to shield ourselves and the world from them? Or, do we decide that we are grown up now? That we can face those things that felt overwhelming in the past? That we can get the help we need to deal with and work through those things that keep us cut off from ourselves? We are each a whole person. We can pretend that we aren't, but the pretending will only last so long.

Today, we will take steps to own and claim all of us. And we will work to figure out what to do with those parts of us that were hidden or disowned. We will gather them to us and start with simple, non-judging, acknowledgment.

Day 1

Close your eyes and think about what you just read. What are the first couple of things you notice about this meditation?

_____

_____

_____

_____

_____

_____

Day 2

Do you remember or know of any things your caregivers had to deny within themselves?

_____

_____

_____

_____

_____

_____

Day 3

What is your first memory of lying to yourself or someone else? How did that feel?

_____

_____

_____

_____

_____

_____

Day 4

Are there things - traits, issues, fears, thoughts, etc. that you try to ignore today?

_____

_____

_____

_____

_____

_____

Day 5

Try this: "I'm afraid if I acknowledge _____,
then _____ will happen." Share your fear with
a trusted other.

_____

_____

_____

_____

_____

_____

Day 6

Try this: "Today, I say 'I love you, and it's going to
be okay' to that part of me I'm afraid to
acknowledge."

_____

_____

_____

_____

_____

_____

Day 7

Reflect on what you have learned about yourself this week.

_____

_____

_____

_____

_____

_____

COMPARING

WEEK 35

We can tell when we are comparing ourselves to another person. When we hear their story, we will either get a sense of judgment or shame. The judgment might sound like, "Really, that's all they did? I could do it better than that." The shame might sound like, "Wow! I could never do that. Look at how wonderful and amazing they seem. I wonder why I've never been able to do something like that? That could never happen for me." Comparing always leads to feeling a little better or a little worse than someone else. It doesn't lead to a balanced appreciation for or recognition of who we are. When we compare ourselves to others, we devalue our humanity and uniqueness. No other person shares our exact set of personality traits, brain pathways, experiences, or life circumstances. It is hurtful to us and others to compare ourselves to them. It takes us out of connection and into separation from others. It robs us of our power, in this moment, to be creative and move toward what we want.

Today, we will refuse to compare ourselves to others. We will notice their positive qualities with love and appreciation. We will do the same for ourselves. We will notice the qualities about them, that are challenging for us, with compassion and grace. We will do the same for ourselves.

Day 1

Close your eyes and think about what you just read. What are the first couple of things you notice about this meditation?

_____

_____

_____

_____

_____

_____

Day 2

When you were young, how did your family speak of others? Was there judgment, acceptance, criticism?

_____

_____

_____

_____

_____

_____

Day 3

Think of a time, earlier in your life - as a teen maybe - when you compared yourself to others. What do you remember about that?

_____

_____

_____

_____

_____

_____

Day 4

Are there times and places, now in your life, that you compare yourself to others? How does that feel?

_____

_____

_____

_____

_____

_____

Day 5

What do you lose when you get preoccupied with comparing yourself to someone?

_____

_____

_____

_____

_____

_____

Day 6

What could you gain if you could notice your comparing, without judging yourself, and then learn to let it go?

_____

_____

_____

_____

_____

_____

Day 7

Reflect on what you have learned about yourself this week.

_____

_____

_____

_____

_____

_____

Grateful

Week 36

s life perfect? Certainly not. Am I merely reveling in lavishness abounding? Nope. Am I without struggles and trials? No way. And… today, I am grateful. I am grateful for my husband who is playful, creative, and always growing. I am grateful for my son who looks at the world from a totally different box. I am grateful for my daughter who handles others with such care. I am grateful for the amazing people that make my work so interesting and rewarding. I am grateful to have walked alongside another human as she passed from this life, as we know it. I am grateful for my friends and family who encourage me, listen to my thoughts and contentions, and speak such kindnesses to me. And I am grateful that my brain and body are allowing me to connect with feelings of gratefulness! I hold onto them gently, knowing that they may pass. There will be days ahead that I am not able to connect with gratefulness. I don't scorn or reject those days - I know that they serve to deepen me and my experience and deepen my ability to appreciate gratefulness.

Today, we will enjoy these feelings of gratefulness.

Day 1

Close your eyes and think about what you just read. What are the first couple of things you notice about this meditation?

_____

_____

_____

_____

_____

_____

Day 2

Did you ever believe the message - "don't enjoy it, it won't last"?

_____

_____

_____

_____

_____

_____

Day 3

Do you believe you could enjoy the pleasantness of gratitude or another emotion, even with the knowledge that it won't last forever?

_____

_____

_____

_____

_____

_____

Day 4

Write down at least several things you are grateful for today.

_____

_____

_____

_____

_____

_____

Day 5

What is scary about savoring a pleasant thought or emotion - knowing it will pass?

_____

_____

_____

_____

_____

_____

Day 6

Practice this affirmation or create your own, "Today I hold my feelings loosely. I love and connect with them, and I allow them to move and pass freely-whether they are pleasant or unpleasant."

Day 7

Reflect on what you learned about yourself this week.

_____

_____

_____

_____

_____

_____

WORTH

WEEK 37

What are we worth? What are our lives worth? Is our worth measured by a number from 1-100? And how would that number be calculated? Is Einstein's life or the Dalai Lama's worth more than mine or yours? What's more important - the heart or the brain? Hearing or sight? A leg or an arm? The truth is, we are all part of humanity - one human race. Just as each organ, sense, or limb is part of one body. Each of us has an influence on one another. Each of us plays an important part. Every life impacts other lives. To erase one life is no small impact on the world. We could wonder who impacted Einstein? Whose influences molded him and led him to be at certain places at certain times?

Whose lives allowed him to connect with certain opportunities? And if "notable" people didn't have the people who influenced them, how would that shift them? Make no mistake - we are a web. Tangled and sticky, at times, but we are a web, nonetheless. Our worth is immeasurable.

Today, we will value ourselves - not only for the raw, observable contribution we make in the world, but for how just being ourselves impacts others, who, in turn, impact others. Our worth is too great to calculate.

Day 1

Close your eyes and think about what you just read. What are the first couple of things you notice about this meditation?

_____

_____

_____

_____

_____

_____

Day 2

Growing up, were all people valued or were some talked about as more or less valuable?

_____

_____

_____

_____

_____

_____

Day 3

What is valuable about who you are? (e.g. I am loving, I am patient, I am smart, I am silly, I am creative, I am driven, I laugh with others, etc.)

_____

_____

_____

_____

_____

_____

Day 4

Name a couple or few people who have benefited from your life - could be your children, could be a friend, could be somebody you helped, etc.

_____

_____

_____

_____

_____

_____

Day 5

The Pyramid Paradigm - If I positively impact 3 people, and they 3, and they 3, that's 39. Let your mind imagine how big your positive impact has been in this world. Notice if you can enjoy that feeling and appreciate yourself a little bit.

_____

_____

_____

_____

_____

Day 6

Name a few people who have positively impacted you. Pause for a moment to be grateful for their contributions to your life.

_____

_____

_____

_____

_____

Day 7

Reflect on what you have learned about yourself this week.

_____

_____

_____

_____

_____

_____

MORE IS MORE

WEEK 38

The world is an abundant place. The more that abundance is shared, the more abundance there is. I was listening to a podcast where they were giving very generous well-wishes for a member of the team who had moved on to another job. The speakers sounded so sincere and exuberant in their message of congratulations. How could they be that happy that someone had moved on and left them? They sounded as if they had no fear that their team member's gain was their loss. But was it really their loss? What happens to us if the people we know are happy, healthy, and wise? Would it be better if they are miserable and lacking? If we are wrestling with an injured sense of self, our friend's misery might help us temporarily. We can make noble comparisons and feel better about ourselves for a while. But the better feeling won't last. And then, we'll be miserable again and surrounded by miserable people. The truth is - fulfilled and generous people have a lot to share with those around them. They have an internal and external resource that pervade the environment close by. And then, we can't help but feel generous and resourced, too. That's how we can tell when we are with people who feel good about who they are – and then we feel good about ourselves, too.

Today, we will give, share, love, and make a point to enjoy and smile when faced with someone else's abundance.

Day 1

Close your eyes and think about what you just read. What are the first couple of things you notice about this meditation?

_____

_____

_____

_____

_____

_____

Day 2

How was the good fortune of others looked upon in your growing up years?

_____

_____

_____

_____

_____

_____

Day 3

Have you noticed times when you are not able to be happy for others' abundance?

_____

_____

_____

_____

_____

_____

Day 4

Have you noticed times when you are able to be happy for others' abundance?

_____

_____

_____

_____

_____

_____

Day 5

What would you need to believe to celebrate for others when they are experiencing goodness in their lives?

_____

_____

_____

_____

_____

_____

Day 6

List 3 positive things you expect to happen in your life. Hope for those things.

_____

_____

_____

_____

_____

_____

Day 7

Reflect on what you have learned about yourself this
week.

_____

_____

_____

_____

_____

_____

OUR STORIES MATTER

WEEK 39

I like to read people's stories. I like to think about what factors and influences led them to be where they are today. I was listening to an interview of a biography writer, and I felt inspired. Why are biographies just for a select group of people? What if every American high schooler had the assignment to write their own autobiography? What if, just for the time they were writing it, they had to stop and think about their lives - who they are to the people who love them; how they came to love dance, singing, juggling, soccer; what things are motivating to them? What are their regrets, losses, and grievances about life? What if every American high schooler had the chance to think about those things and then had the opportunity to share and talk about some of those things? Then I think about the value there is for each of us in telling our stories. Just putting words on paper or saying something out loud gives us a different perspective than when those thoughts are just roaming around in our heads. I'm not saying anyone would pay to read my story - but value is often not about money. I know my story matters significantly to at least a couple of handfuls of people. It makes me who I am, and I, along with you my fellow humans, have tremendous value in this world. Telling our stories is a little like studying history. It gives us the opportunity to reflect, consider, and learn from our past. It gives us an opportunity to approach our future with intention.

Today, let us take a moment to pause and say out loud or write down a part of our stories.

Day 1

Close your eyes and think about what you just read. What are the first couple of things you notice about this meditation?

_____

_____

_____

_____

_____

_____

Day 2

What influences made your primary caregivers who they were? What are their stories?

_____

_____

_____

_____

_____

_____

Day 3

Think about your early life influences. What are some of those influences? (e.g. what beliefs and values did your family hold that led to your early beliefs and values? What did being in your family teach you about yourself? What is your most important early childhood memory?)

_____

_____

_____

_____

_____

Day 4

When you think about your story, what are a few things you have wished could have been different?

_____

_____

_____

_____

_____

Day 5

What are a few things you are grateful for, in your life story?

_____

_____

_____

_____

_____

_____

Day 6

If you were starting a new chapter today, what would you title it?

_____

_____

_____

_____

_____

_____

Day 7

What did you learn about yourself this week?

_____

_____

_____

_____

_____

_____

LET'S PLAY

WEEK 40

D id you ever have the ability, as a child, to get fully immersed in the activity at hand? Throwing rocks in the creek, playing with dolls, riding a bike, playing with the dog, or cops & robbers? Most young children have that ability. And then we adults start training them out of play as soon as we can - "put your shoes on now; stop playing, it's time to eat; I need you to focus on this now; don't follow that bubble, we have to go now." Well, what are we supposed to do? That's the way our world works. I always knew, growing up, that work was more valued than play, but, I had never seen it more blatantly labeled in black and white than yesterday. I was reading a children's biography of a scientist.

One of the historical notes was that the Puritans believed that children needed their parents' permission to play. Seriousness was valued. Harsh punishment for stepping out of the boundaries was encouraged. It became so clear to me in that instant. Many of us Americans were raised, through generational transmission and a range of subtle cues, to believe people who are playful aren't as valuable as those who work hard. If you **have** to play as a child, then fine. But you had better start outgrowing it as soon as possible. Get serious. Get prepared. Life is a lot of hard work and planning and preparing. Then, if you plan and prepare enough, one day, you can relax. Phew - I'm exhausted just thinking about it! Fortunately, for us who are living now, there is plenty of research that shows that happiness and playfulness are important factors for creativity and productivity. Nurturing a couple of deep relationships and making time on a regular basis for activities of pure enjoyment go a long way toward living a healthy, productive, and (dare I say) even spiritual life.

Today, we will pick one thing and do it just for fun - just for the enjoyment. We will immerse ourselves in it.

Day 1

Close your eyes and think about what you just read. What are the first couple of things you notice about this meditation?

_____

_____

_____

_____

_____

_____

Day 2

When you think about taking time to play, what are all the different possibilities that come to mind? Which ones are you most drawn to?

_____

_____

_____

_____

_____

_____

Day 3

Pencil 3 playtimes (at least 30 minutes) into the next week of your calendar - then follow through, barring anything catastrophic.

_____

_____

_____

_____

_____

_____

Day 4

What were the attitudes toward work and play when you were growing up?

_____

_____

_____

_____

_____

_____

Day 5

Do you come close to a balance of work and play, now in your life?

_____

_____

_____

_____

_____

_____

Day 6

Does play come easily or do you feel a sense of disease about it?

_____

_____

_____

_____

_____

_____

Day 7

Reflect on what you learned about yourself this week.

_____

_____

_____

_____

_____

_____

Yin Yang

Week 41

Beauty and blessing, struggle and trial. Life is full of juxtapositions. Where would we be without one or the other? Perhaps without struggle and trial, we would be completely self-centered, incapable of cooperating and working together to nourish life. Without blessing and beauty, we would surely be in a world of hurt, literally. Today, I am grateful for the balance of these things. I am grateful that I can plunge into the depths of despair with a friend and then turn and soar into a flight of joy over life's simple pleasures like dancing in the living room, a piece of chocolate, or laughing about something funny with family.

Today, may we all be blessed with gratitude for the simple yin yang of which we are a part.

Day 1

Close your eyes and think about what you just read. What are the first couple of things you notice about this meditation?

_____

_____

_____

_____

_____

_____

Day 2

How were struggles and trials viewed in your home, growing up? Were they seen as a normal part of life to be met with readiness? Were you allowed to grieve the pain of struggle?

_____

_____

_____

_____

_____

Day 3

How were joy and celebration viewed in your home?
Was it looked for and nourished?

_____

_____

_____

_____

_____

_____

Day 4

What do you say to others when they are in a time of
trial - do you feel helpful at those times?

_____

_____

_____

_____

_____

_____

Day 5

Create a greeting that you would like to practice when times of struggle come along - e.g. Hello struggle. I am listening, and I want to learn all I can. I know this will help me develop more fully in _____ area.

_____

_____

_____

_____

_____

Day 6

Create a greeting that you would like to practice when times of joy and blessing come along - e.g. Hello joy! Thank you for coming. I revel in you and in this _____ that is happening right now!

_____

_____

_____

_____

_____

Day 7

Reflect on what you have learned about yourself this week.

_____

_____

_____

_____

_____

_____

SEE THE VISION

WEEK 42

If there is a way in which you want to grow today, if there is progress or maturation that you are longing for, then be courageous and imagine yourself possessing that trait or quality. See yourself living that growth you would like to have. I was inspired by the story "Left To Tell" by Immaculee Ilibagiza. After surviving the Rwandan Holocaust, she set her mind to finding a job. There were very few jobs to find, but she said, "I envisioned it, I dreamed it, I prayed for it, and now, I had it!". Neuroscience backs her up. When we envision something, like being at the ocean, the same neural circuitry lights up as if we were actually staring at it! So live big. Your imagination is the limit. Set your sights high. Whether it is embodying patience with your children or learning to paint - allow the desire you feel for that growth to motivate you. Then repeatedly imagine yourself engaging with life in that new way. After some time and practice, you may be very pleasantly surprised.

Today, we will envision in ourselves a trait or quality we want to possess.

Day 1

Close your eyes and think about what you just read. What are the first couple of things you notice about this meditation?

_____

_____

_____

_____

_____

_____

Day 2

Did your family view life more as full of opportunity or full of limitation?

_____

_____

_____

_____

_____

_____

Day 3

What is something you have always wanted to do or a trait you have always wanted to possess, but were afraid to acknowledge and hope for?

_____

_____

_____

_____

_____

_____

Day 4

Name the fear - e.g. I'm afraid if I go for this, and it doesn't happen, then that says _____ about me or my life."

_____

_____

_____

_____

_____

_____

Day 5

Create a positive self-statement - e.g., "I am setting my intention on this, and I fully expect that I will realize this _____." (You probably won't believe yourself at first - that's ok. Keep saying it. You will create the neural networks to support it." Or as some would say, "Fake it till you make it.")

_____

_____

_____

_____

_____

Day 6

Practice your positive self-statement.

_____

_____

_____

_____

_____

_____

Day 7

Reflect on what you have learned about yourself this week.

_____

_____

_____

_____

_____

_____

FACE THE HILL

WEEK 43

Crisis points, inflection points, points of major change aren't bad, even though they will probably be uncomfortable. Often, they are uncomfortable. Think of starting a new habit with your body - a stretch, jogging, or climbing a hill. Your body is going to speak to you and let you know that this is out of character and difficult. Your body is going to warn you to check it out and make sure you want to go ahead with it. And if you evaluate it, and decide that the effort has value and merit, you go ahead with it. Sometimes we don't get a choice about whether a change is coming - like in times of crisis. We have to climb the hill - one way or another. But we always get a choice about how we climb.

How we choose to speak and think about it are in our control. We can tell the story as if this is the worst hill that ever came along, and it will ruin our lives. Or we can tell the story as if this hill is hard, difficult, and painful, but we know we'll get through it in a meaningful way. We can also be good to ourselves as we climb. We can stop and stretch or take a water break along the way. We know that we will learn something and grow. We have that capacity as adults. If no one modeled that for us, then we didn't have that capacity as children. But life is always presenting us with opportunities to grow those young parts of ourselves. The crisis points and hills are redundancies built in to allow us to learn this time, what we may not have been able to learn before.

Today, we will find joy in the opportunity to grow to our fullest potential by courageously facing the hills.

Day 1

Close your eyes and think about what you just read. What are the first couple of things you notice about this meditation?

_____

_____

_____

_____

_____

_____

Day 2

How did your family view crises and hard times as you were growing up?

_____

_____

_____

_____

_____

_____

Day 3

What was a difficult time in your life that you are still struggling to understand?

_____

_____

_____

_____

_____

_____

Day 4

What was a difficult time in your life you value, knowing how much it taught you?

_____

_____

_____

_____

_____

_____

Day 5

What belief would you like to hold onto for when difficult times come along? E.g. All things in my life will work to bring about good for me, even uncomfortable things.

_____

_____

_____

_____

_____

Day 6

Write down a few things you can do for self-comfort when difficult times come. E.g. Talk to a friend, make my favorite cup of tea, pray, visit nature, etc.

_____

_____

_____

_____

_____

_____

Day 7

Reflect on what you have learned about yourself this week.

_____

_____

_____

_____

_____

_____

THE THREE LOVES

WEEK 44

What is love? Does love mean feeling a certain way for someone? Does love mean certain things you do? Can you hurt someone and still love them? Where does love come from and how do we know when it's "real"? When does love begin and end? I wish the answers to these questions were clear cut. I wish these questions could be answered in as clear and non-murky a way as two plus two. Love is certainly about the heart. It's that warm, full feeling. And love is certainly also about care and respect and commitment and honesty. Love is all of these things and more. Love is very powerful. I wonder how many poems, songs, sonnets, plays, books, and tragedies have been written about love? I wonder why we humans are so infatuated with love? From a purely physiological perspective, you wouldn't think love necessary for a human to grow physically. But infants who don't have a loving touch can stop thriving and die, even if they have food and a clean diaper. I guess love is a biological imperative. I guess we really can't get by without it.

I think we get confused when we adults expect that loving someone else and being loved by someone else will complete us and make us whole. The truth is, loving others is an important component of love, but it is just one component. The other two main components are spiritual love (receiving boundless love from the universe, God, the earth - however you conceive of your source) and self-love. Those three components must be in balance for us to evolve toward wholeness. It is with the balance of these three loves that we thrive. When we have balanced love, we can feel and demonstrate the different properties that comprise love.

To be balanced in love, we focus on receiving love from our source and allowing ourselves to be filled with love. Then we enjoy and cherish that experience of being loved. Lastly, we allow that love to spill over onto those around us. We won't feel like being loving every minute, but we receive enough to help us love most of the time. We are human and imperfect. We are not able to love perfectly, continuously. That's okay. Hopefully, others are in a state of growth, too, and can show up with their love when we are struggling.

Today, we will pay attention to balance in the 3 areas of love (spiritual love, self-love, and other love).

Day 1

Close your eyes and think about what you just read.
What are the first couple of things you notice about
this meditation?

_____

_____

_____

_____

_____

_____

Day 2

What are some of the messages you learned about
love, growing up?

_____

_____

_____

_____

_____

_____

Day 3

Which love do you find hardest to connect with - spiritual, self, or other love, and why?

_____

_____

_____

_____

_____

_____

Day 4

Which love is the easiest for you to connect with - spiritual, self, or other love, and why?

_____

_____

_____

_____

_____

_____

Day 5

Have you ever had unrealistic expectations about being loved by others - that it would be enough that you wouldn't need the other two loves?

_____

_____

_____

_____

_____

Day 6

Think of how you could connect with each of the three loves today - e.g. going for a walk in nature (spiritual), soaking in a warm bath (self-love), passing along or taking in some kind words (love with others).

_____

_____

_____

_____

_____

Day 7

Reflect on what you have learned about yourself this week.

_____

_____

_____

_____

_____

_____

Bitterness

Week 45

You dare not drink of bitterness - it blackens the soul and leaves you bankrupt and empty. It robs of joy and hope. It divides families and cuts off healthy hopes and dreams at the knees - to leave you maimed and hobbling. It is a sour poison that violently attacks the one swallowing the pill. Though your mind may be infatuated, safe, and secure when dancing with it, the body will weaken, atrophy, and die. Oh bitterness, go away. Don't be a bother anymore. Be gone and leave behind freedom and peace. Leave, instead, wholeness and happiness. Leave these blessed ones to connection, contentment, and love. If you should find yourself entertaining bitterness, turn to the bitter thought, love the original hurt part of self, forgive the bitterness root and the one who caused it, and then declare "no more." Summon the sharp instrument and sever it. Have a memorial, burn it, and spread the ashes -left to foster new life. Green growth, come. Tender shoots break forth! Opportunity, hope, and vision rise.

Today, we will take care to prune out any roots of bitterness.

Day 1

Close your eyes and think about what you just read. What are the first couple of things you notice about this meditation?

_____

_____

_____

_____

_____

_____

Day 2

How did your family deal with old hurts and wounds as you were growing up?

_____

_____

_____

_____

_____

_____

Day 3

Have you had any times in your life when you clung to bitterness?

_____

_____

_____

_____

_____

_____

Day 4

Have you had times when you have been able to let go of bitterness?

_____

_____

_____

_____

_____

_____

Day 5

Is there anyone in your life who is good at not holding grudges, not getting resentful, letting things go? Imagine how that feels.

_____

_____

_____

_____

_____

_____

Day 6

Is there any bitterness that you are holding today that you would like to let go of? Don't be afraid to repeat the letting go again and again. Sometimes it feels instant, sometimes it doesn't.

_____

_____

_____

_____

_____

Day 7

Reflect on what you have learned about yourself this
week.

_____

_____

_____

_____

_____

_____

CONFESSIONS

WEEK 46

'm reading a book about forgiveness. The author encourages confessing flaws and weaknesses as a part of living a full life. Once we get past the discomfort, it sure is freeing to own our humanness. To freely and openly admit our weaknesses, failings, and shortcomings. To embody each of these is to be perfectly human. Denying and defending weaknesses makes us sick. It makes us hide with shame. It makes us need to separate ourselves into "us and them." Denial makes us compare ourselves to others. So here goes - as I intend to live in the wholeness and fullness of my human capacity - I still fall short in these and other areas: jealousy, anger, unforgiveness, grouchiness, impatience, judgmentalness, pickiness, and stubbornness. I confess that I have caused harm to others through these and other short-comings. I rejoice that if I am accused of these things, I can say, "yes, you are right!" I resolve not to manipulate, defend, or otherwise attempt to misdirect the responsibility for these things. I am human! And I am grateful that I am loved, appreciated, and cared for in spite of all of these flaws. And I am grateful that I can also own and appreciate my patience, kindness, care for others, wisdom, and hardiness. Being human is such as interesting journey, and I am constantly intrigued.

Today, we will try our hand at confessions- maybe to a journal, maybe to God, maybe to another person.

Day 1

Close your eyes and think about what you just read.
What are the first couple of things you notice about
this meditation?

_____

_____

_____

_____

_____

_____

Day 2

Were your parents able to admit their mistakes and
weaknesses?

_____

_____

_____

_____

_____

_____

Day 3

What do you find the hardest to admit about yourself?

_____

_____

_____

_____

_____

_____

Day 4

What things are easy for you to own and claim about yourself?

_____

_____

_____

_____

_____

_____

Day 5

What good things do you need to be able to believe about yourself to admit your weaknesses? E.g. I am loved no matter what, I am in good company, with every other human who is just as flawed as me, etc.

_____

_____

_____

_____

_____

_____

Day 6

Make a confession, here and now today.

_____

_____

_____

_____

_____

_____

Day 7

Reflect on what you learned about yourself this week.

_____

_____

_____

_____

_____

_____

PAST, FUTURE, PRESENT

WEEK 47

I hope that you find some meaning in today. I hope you find a way to enjoy yourself today - to connect with someone you love, to breathe in and breathe out a bit of goodness that is right in front of you. Maybe you find beauty in nature. Maybe you enjoy a friend. Maybe you read something meaningful. For the past is only stored, and the future is only imagined. Hold on loosely to them. Yes, we remember and acknowledge. Yes, we plan. And yes, we need to remain open to the possibilities unfolding right here, right now.

Today, we will go easy on ourselves. We will breathe in and breathe out and know that we are ok in this moment right now. We have what we need to get through this moment, and we allow ourselves to experience pleasure and enjoyment in that.

Day 1

Close your eyes and think about what you just read. What are the first couple of things you notice about this meditation?

_____

_____

_____

_____

_____

_____

Day 2

In your home, growing up, was there any worry for the future or regret or romanticizing of the past?

_____

_____

_____

_____

_____

_____

Day 3

How is it for you now, when you try to enjoy the present moment?

_____

_____

_____

_____

_____

_____

Day 4

What is your biggest worry for the future? How could you comfort yourself? E.g. I have gotten to this point, and I know that I will get through whatever comes.

_____

_____

_____

_____

_____

_____

Day 5

What is your biggest regret or fantasy of the past? How could you calm yourself about that? E.g. The past is not happening now - it is only a stored memory. I let go of needing it to be different or needing to re-create it.

_____

_____

_____

_____

_____

Day 6

Take a moment to be very present-oriented. Set a two-minute timer and notice what is happening right here and right now. See how that is. E.g. I notice my feet planted on the floor, my back against the seat cushions, my breath flowing in and out, the sound of the clock ticking, the water as it touches my lips and flows over my tongue and down my throat.

_____

_____

_____

_____

_____

_____

Day 7

Reflect on what you have learned about yourself this week.

_____

_____

_____

_____

_____

_____

EMBRACE FAILURE

WEEK 48

Embrace failure as a part of life's important journeys. Failure is an important part of success. It is how each of us, who knows how to walk, learned to do it. Failure is how each of us, who knows how to ride a bike, learned to do it. We failed, and we failed, and we succeeded just a little, and we kept on. Then, at some point, we had success. Failure means that you have tried something and learned from it. Failure means that you have set your sights higher. Sometimes, when we set our sights high, we get afraid. We may be overcome by "what ifs" - e.g. What if I fail? If we are afraid of failure, what do we do? How do we adults, who forgot we learned to walk, get ourselves to face those fears?

One thing we can do is reward failure! When you try something and fail, you deserve to pat yourself on the back and say, "good job, you took that as far as you could, way to go! Nice work, you found the edge of that idea." You also can say to yourself, "well, you did a poor job at (fill in the blank), now you have an opportunity to make a connection by apologizing and finding out how that could go differently," whoopee! What if we really valued and praised our failures? Think of all the things we might try. Not all failures are alike - some failures will be painful for a long time. That's ok. Usually, those bring about really important deepening and knowledge. But there are many possibilities that seem more doable when we embrace failure.

Today, we will try something in a new or different way and embrace our failures joyfully.

Day 1

Close your eyes and think about what you just read. What are the first couple of things you notice about this meditation?

_____

_____

_____

_____

_____

_____

Day 2

What beliefs did you develop early in your life about failure?

_____

_____

_____

_____

_____

_____

Day 3

What has been a failure in your life that still bothers you?

_____

_____

_____

_____

_____

_____

Day 4

What has been a failure in your life, which has brought important learning?

_____

_____

_____

_____

_____

_____

Day 5

Create an affirmation for the failure that bothers you.
E.g. Even though I failed at _____, I know I did
the best I could get myself to do at the time. I forgive
myself. I really learned _____.

_____

_____

_____

_____

_____

_____

Day 6

Write down one or two things you could try this
week, knowing that you are risking failure.

_____

_____

_____

_____

_____

_____

Day 7

Reflect on what you have learned about yourself this week.

_____

_____

_____

_____

_____

_____

Embracing True Wealth

Week 49

'm always moved when people come together to do something, where the primary goal isn't about personal gain. It's hard. We look around us and see that we could have this or that if we were rich. We think if we hang onto all that we have and strive to get more, we will be closer to being rich. But what is rich, anyway? Is it $100K per year? Is it when your passive income exceeds your living needs? Is it when you can retire? Is it a certain number of trophies or awards? What if rich is when you are engaged in something meaningful, that makes your heart happy. Maybe rich is when you know you can weather any storm in a relationship. Maybe rich is when you can see the good your gift has done in someone's life.

Maybe rich is when you take one step toward a goal you have for your life. Maybe rich is when you have a passion and are able to engage in that passion, while simultaneously using it to connect with and serve others. Maybe when we are rich in those ways, we will be able to relax about personal gain. Maybe then we stop and say, "One of my primary goals is to have a positive impact on my world - my sphere of influence." Maybe that supports us in coming together to do something that isn't primarily about personal gain. So maybe our letting go of the goal of constant personal gain makes us rich, after all.

Today, we will engage in an activity where our primary goal is gain for someone or something other than us, without losing connection with ourselves, in the process.

Day 1

Close your eyes and think about what you just read. What are the first couple of things you notice about this meditation?

Day 2

What was your family's view of wealth and giving, growing up?

Day 3

What are times you have felt really generous in your life?

_____

_____

_____

_____

_____

_____

Day 4

When are times you felt you had nothing to give?

_____

_____

_____

_____

_____

_____

Day 5

How do you suppose we find a balance in giving - to ourselves and others? What would that look like in your life?

_____

_____

_____

_____

_____

_____

Day 6

Define what wealth means to you in your life. E.g. I know I am, or I feel wealthy when _____.

_____

_____

_____

_____

_____

_____

Day 7

Reflect on what you have learned about yourself this week.

_____

_____

_____

_____

_____

_____

Praise, Thanksgiving, Confession, and Supplication

Week 50

I f you are a Bible reader, you might recognize these title words as instructions about how to come to God. But even if you are a non-Bible reader, or have no religious beliefs whatsoever, I think these words are extremely applicable to most relationships in our lives. Often, we get into patterns about how we approach those close to us - "did you do the dishes? Are you finished yet? Stop that!" And there are going to be many times when we rely on those shorthand patterns to save time or get something accomplished. But what if we were also to make time and space for some praise, thanksgiving, confession, and supplication? I wonder what impact we could have on the tone and growth of our relationships. Let's look at how that might sound: "You are really a wonderful cook (praise). Thank you for a good dinner(thanksgiving). I am sometimes envious of how you can put things together and make them taste so good (confession). I was also wondering if we might be able to eat at 5:30 instead of 6:00? It would help me make it to my meeting on time (supplication)." The shorthand is - "could we eat at 5:30 instead of 6:00 to help me get to my meeting on time?" There's nothing wrong with that statement, but which statement do you think will lend itself more to positive feelings in the relationship? The PTCS pattern will help us remember to build up our relationships. It will help us put some effort and energy into nurturing the other person. Sometimes we only have time for the shorthand, but I bet we could make some time for PTCS, too. Incidentally, if we are re-parenting ourselves, we can use this pattern. Yes, I am encouraging you to talk to yourself! To self - "You are a really wonderful organizer. Thank you for getting me to all my appointments on time. I know I don't always leave enough time for relaxing. Would you help me make better use of my schedule to create some downtime?"

Today, we will nurture our relationships with ourselves and others by utilizing the PTCS pattern.

Day 1

Close your eyes and think about what you just read. What are the first couple of things you notice about this meditation?

_____

_____

_____

_____

_____

_____

Day 2

How were people approached in your home growing up?

_____

_____

_____

_____

_____

_____

Day 3

What are your strengths of communication with your loved ones?

_____

_____

_____

_____

_____

_____

Day 4

What are areas of weakness of communication with your loved ones?

_____

_____

_____

_____

_____

_____

Day 5

Try the PTCS a couple times today.

_____

_____

_____

_____

_____

_____

Day 6

Having tried the PTCS, what do you think? How did it feel? If it was new, it might be uncomfortable. (If you forgot or avoided it, try it today.)

_____

_____

_____

_____

_____

_____

Day 7

What did you learn about yourself this week?

_____

_____

_____

_____

_____

_____

TRUST

WEEK 51

What can we do but trust? What choice do we have? Things in life will come along - struggles, problems, choices, and good times. Each of these things will come and go regardless of how "good" we are or how "bad" we've been, regardless of how successful, rich, beautiful, or motivated we are or are not. The control we have in life is to trust that all is happening as it should be and to choose how we respond. We can kick and scream and drag our heals as a child does, or we can open our hearts to love, support, and the connections that come through struggle. We can relax into the ride. We will still have emotions. We will still feel the sting of life. That is okay. Having emotions isn't what determines our response or how we move through. Trust is one practice that helps us move through life in a way that builds us up instead of tearing us down. Trust helps us maintain our optimism and know that whatever we are experiencing is here to make us deeper and, ultimately, our lives richer.

Today, we will trust that whatever is happening is meant to be - just for us. We will trust that what is, is far better than what we could have planned for ourselves. We will say out loud - "We trust that this will end up for the best."

Day 1

Close your eyes and think about what you just read. What are the first couple of things you notice about this meditation?

_____

_____

_____

_____

_____

_____

Day 2

How did your family, growing up, view life's struggles? What were the messages given about why people struggle?

_____

_____

_____

_____

_____

_____

Day 3

Have you ever judged yourself when you were having a hard time or struggling?

_____

_____

_____

_____

_____

_____

Day 4

Can you look back over your life and see times where struggling led to something good in your life? E.g. growth, a new relationship, letting go of a difficult relationship, a broader perspective, more empathy...

_____

_____

_____

_____

_____

Day 5

Is there an area of your life with which you are struggling that you would like to be able to relax and let go?

_____

_____

_____

_____

_____

_____

Day 6

Create an affirmation for yourself - e.g. "Today, I choose to approach _____ with an open hand. I will neither push away or cling to _____."

_____

_____

_____

_____

_____

_____

Day 7

Reflect on what you have learned about yourself this week.

_____

_____

_____

_____

_____

_____

Evidence of Love

Week 52

'm watching a movie about Mother Teresa and her work among the poor in Calcutta. What an amazing story! What's even more amazing is that most people understand who you are talking about when you refer to "Mother Teresa." Her work was meaningful on at least two levels. One was the direct contact she had with poor, hurting people. The fact that they didn't have to be alone in their suffering as they died. She treated them as worthy and deserving, even though they were considered the least deserving by their own people. The other level is how her actions speak to the rest of us as evidence of love. Anytime you are hurting, and question whether there is love in this world, or whether you are deserving of that love, think of Mother Teresa. We probably aren't as financially poor as the people she worked with in Calcutta, but sometimes we can be very poor in spirit. Sometimes we feel, metaphorically, like those people who were left alone to die in the streets. We can imagine Mother Teresa's love comforting us. Imagine her saying, "it's ok, you're not alone now, I'm here."

Today, we will remind ourselves that we are not alone. That love is here and all around. We will remember the evidence of love, shown by Mother Teresa.

Day 1

Close your eyes and think about what you just read. What are the first couple of things you notice about this meditation?

_____

_____

_____

_____

_____

_____

Day 2

In your family of origin, was there an abundance of love to go around? Did you sometimes feel that there wasn't enough? Did you feel connected to in times of distress or need?

_____

_____

_____

_____

_____

Day 3

To whom/ under what circumstances is it easy for you to give love?

_____

_____

_____

_____

_____

_____

Day 4

To whom/ under what circumstances is it difficult for you to give love?

_____

_____

_____

_____

_____

_____

Day 5

Write about how it feels to receive love. Sometimes it might be easy, while sometimes it might be difficult.

_____

_____

_____

_____

_____

_____

Day 6

Today, imagine Mother Teresa's love (or someone in your life who is a Mother Teresa-like person) being directed at you. How does that feel?

_____

_____

_____

_____

_____

_____

Day 7

Reflect on what you have learned about yourself this week.

_____

_____

_____

_____

_____

_____

UNDERSTOOD

BONUS 1

How do we get through tough places in this life? How do we hang onto intimacy within, in a world that beckons us to lose ourselves in pleasure, play, money, busyness, knowledge, productivity, parenting, etc.? How do we remain true to our own inner values, passions, and needs, and not let so many highly visible opinions and trends tell us who we need to be and how we need to live? Well, there are probably many strategies. One strategy strikes me as the powerful experience of being understood. It just happened to me this morning. I was sharing about a place of vulnerability, struggle, and discovery. My listener let me know that she really heard me. Her words wrapped me in a delicate, light and airy, comforting sheathe. She reflected to me that she found value in my struggle and encouraged me that my struggle was worthwhile and beneficial. I felt understood. Her words did not solve my problem. They did not give me 3 easy steps for overcoming the difficulty. They did not promise relief from the challenge. They merely and miraculously confronted me with the reality that she heard and understood where I was, in that moment. And that was just what I needed to help me hold onto the part of myself that was struggling.

Today, we will watch for moments where we feel powerfully understood, and we will watch for opportunities to do that with others.

Day 1

Close your eyes and think about what you just read. What are the first couple of things you notice about this meditation?

_____

_____

_____

_____

_____

Day 2

Growing up, did you have the sense that you were really listened to and understood? Or perhaps, you were given a quick platitude or possible solution instead? Perhaps you couldn't share your feelings at all?

_____

_____

_____

_____

_____

Day 3

Are there any times you remember not being listened to when you really needed it?

_____

_____

_____

_____

_____

_____

Day 4

Are there any times you remember somebody taking the time to listen and understand that made you feel valued and validated?

_____

_____

_____

_____

_____

_____

Day 5

Do you know what it feels like to claim yourself, stay with yourself, hold onto yourself, in the midst of a struggle? Can you see how having someone really listen to you could help you do that?

_____

_____

_____

_____

_____

Day 6

Today, when a loved one talks, make a deliberate effort to listen and let them know you value their experience.

_____

_____

_____

_____

_____

_____

Day 7

Reflect on what you have learned about yourself this week.

_____

_____

_____

_____

_____

_____

HOLD

BONUS 2

Can I accept myself fully, all of who I am? It's a bit of a scary question. When I dig deep, when I catch glimpses of those parts of myself from which I sometimes hide, can I really and truly draw in and embrace those parts of me? Can I say that, no matter what, I won't reject myself? I won't turn on myself. I won't leave myself lonely, out in the cold, and hurting without comfort? I have not always understood that kind of love. The love I understood was far more conditional - I feel loved if I perform this way or look that way or say the right things. In my young, underdeveloped brain, that's how I understood the world. Over time, with lots of healing, adapting, and creating flexibility, I have come to understand that I really can practice unconditional love with myself. That no matter how someone else is frustrated with me, not understanding me, or even attacking me, I can hold onto myself. And when the voices of my own past, that reverberate inside me, seek to attack me - even then - I can hold onto myself. I can love those parts of myself too. It all comes from pain. And if I hold on, and refuse to let go, I can heal the pain.

Today, we will practice awareness of the most ashamed and hurt parts of ourselves, and we will hold them.

Day 1

Close your eyes and think about what you just read. What are the first couple of things you notice about this meditation?

_____

_____

_____

_____

_____

_____

Day 2

In what ways was love conditional or unconditional when you were growing up?

_____

_____

_____

_____

_____

_____

Day 3

Are there ways in which you have shown conditional love with yourself?

_____

_____

_____

_____

_____

Day 4

What does it mean to you to love yourself? Think of the ways in which you enjoy showing love to others - do you do those things for yourself? Think of how your heart swells when you think of someone you love - does your heart do that when you think of you?

_____

_____

_____

_____

_____

Day 5

Are there times when you have really loved yourself, and that felt good?

_____

_____

_____

_____

_____

_____

Day 6

Intentionally practice an act of kindness and love toward yourself this week.

_____

_____

_____

_____

_____

_____

Day 7

Reflect on what you learned about yourself this week.

_____

_____

_____

_____

_____

_____

THEORETICALLY UNLOVABLE

BONUS 3

I f doing good, being loving, and being successful is what makes people lovable, then we are all *theoretically* unlovable because we just can't do it all the time. Sometimes we can't do it most of the time. And if those things are what gives humans value and worth, then what about babies? Why do we love babies? What have they done to earn any value or worth? What certificates have they achieved, or performances mastered that we should love them or call them valuable? How have they earned their keep or demonstrated mutuality in a relationship? I think you can see the absurdity there. Of course, babies haven't done anything to earn our love - they are just worthy of love by virtue of being born. As are we all. That does not give us a license to freely be unkind or unjust or always taking. It is to say that - no matter how deplorable our actions have been - we all deserve for someone to see through all of that, right to the core that we were born with, and say "I see you in there, and you are lovable." When I act unlovable, there is always a reason. There is always something driving me to act in that way. And that wound needs healing. We all have those areas. It isn't a bad thing that we struggle and miss the boat with one another. It does feel bad. But if we can take that bad feeling and use it to motivate us toward growth and healing, then we've gained a lot. Using our deeds, performances, accomplishments, achievements as the sole or main way to gain lovableness will fail us. If those are the bulk of our measures, then we are, *theoretically*, unlovable. But, if we remember the tender, vulnerable, hurting, damaged and even joyous parts within us and say that we are lovable because those places need love, then what a different picture! Babies are lovable because they need us to love them, and so are we. We are lovable because we need love.

Today, we will stop trying to earn love by being good. We will love ourselves and others because we need love - and that makes us *theoretically* lovable.

Day 1

Close your eyes and think about what you just read. What are the first couple of things you notice about this meditation?

_____

_____

_____

_____

_____

_____

Day 2

Were there any conditions to being lovable when you were growing up?

_____

_____

_____

_____

_____

_____

Day 3

Are there any conditions, for being lovable, that you have placed on yourself?

_____

_____

_____

_____

_____

_____

Day 4

Are there conditions, for being lovable, that you have placed on others in your life?

_____

_____

_____

_____

_____

_____

Day 5

Have conditions of being lovable cost you peace with yourself or others?

_____

_____

_____

_____

_____

_____

Day 6

Are there any conditions for loving yourself that you would like to let go of, e.g. "I let go of needing to check everything off my list, lose weight, make my parents happy, get a Ph.D., etc. in order to be lovable."

_____

_____

_____

_____

_____

Day 7

Reflect on what you have learned about yourself this week.

_____

_____

_____

_____

_____

_____

Endings

Bonus 4

Endings are a mixed bag. They signify that something is coming to a closure. It is terminating. We are moving on. There can be all kinds of feelings that go along with endings - sometimes relief and joy, sometimes pain, sadness, guilt, or anger. Each of those feelings is just fine. What we feel is what we feel. Is it how we respond to our feelings that determines our healing path. Do we judge and hide our feelings, or do we love and respect our feelings? Can we be open to moving through whatever feelings arise in response to an ending? We may choose not to act on many of our feelings. And every feeling is an opportunity for us to come to know and express the unique and wonderful people we are.

Today, we will embrace and nurture all our feelings related to endings.

Reflect on what you have learned about yourself this year.

As this book ends, I hope that you have learned how to develop an open, accepting, and loving relationship with yourself and others leading to a sense of connection greater than yourself. I hope that you have found some tools, thought patterns, and methods for making sense of our everyday life experiences. And I hope that you will be able to practice, integrate, and incorporate some of these tools as you move forward in your life. I hope you feel it is possible for you to continuing growing and developing throughout your lifetime! May you be well. May you have peace. May you be happy.

URGENT PLEA!

Thank You For Reading My Book!

I really appreciate all of your feedback, and I love hearing what you have to say.

I need your input to make the next version of this book and my future books even better.

Please leave me a helpful review on Amazon letting me know what you thought of the book.

Thank you so much!

~ Jennifer Onstot, MA, MFT